# Policeman's Patrol

Harry Cole was born and brought up in Bermondsey, south London. He left school when he was fourteen, during the war, and became a cricket-bat maker, soldier, stonemason and, in 1952, a policeman. For thirty years, until his retirement in 1983, he served at the same police station in London.

He is a qualified FA coach (he has run numerous junior football teams), a referee and a keen cricketer. For many years he had a regular column in the *Warren*, the police magazine. His other books are *Policeman's Progress*, *Policeman's Lot*, *Policeman's Patch*, *Policeman's Prelude* and *Policeman's Story*, his two-volume autobiography, *Policeman's Gazette* and *The Blue Apprentices*, a novel.

In 1978 Harry Cole was awarded the British Empire Medal for voluntary work. Since leaving the force, in addition to writing he has taken up after-dinner speaking.

Harry Cole

# Policeman's Patrol

FONTANA/Collins

First published in Great Britain
in 1983 by Fontana Paperbacks,
8 Grafton Street, London W1X 3LA
Fourth impression May 1988

Printed and bound in Great Britain by
William Collins Sons & Co. Ltd, Glasgow

The views expressed in this book are the author's own
and do not necessarily reflect the official views of
the Metropolitan Police

To the men and women of
Carter Street Police Station,
the 'Wharf Road'

# Contents

## Derby Day

There was no doubt about it, it was going to be an absolute scorcher. It was barely eight o'clock and already the sun was heavy on our shoulders. Twenty constables (including one young lady named Celia), two sergeants and an inspector were about to have a day out. And what a day out! All over London coaches were being given a final spit and polish before they began their long round of pubs, clubs, old folk's homes, factories and offices. Pick-ups would be made at just about every type of building except undertakers' and prisons. Milkmen scurried through their rounds glaring at notes that ordered extra pintas. Postmen pushed letters through flaps with a zest that took the envelopes halfway up passages. Villains stopped villainy, road-menders stopped working and grandmothers were buried by the thousands. Today was Derby Day!

Epsom race course is on the fringe of the Metropolitan Police area and it must be all of fifteen miles from Wharf Road Police Station. A copper could spend all of his service in central London and never once be lucky enough to make it to the Derby. Well, here I was, in my last year of service, and I had finally wangled my way on to the list. It is true that we were all on duty and not Derby-bound for any social outing, but it would need to be some real calamity that would ruin *this* day.

The police coach stopped just outside our police station

and the Wharf Road contingent climbed aboard. There we joined twenty-three other officers from Peckham and Tower Bridge. Traffic was already building up and it took just over an hour to travel the fifteen miles to the course. Later in the morning it would take nearer three.

The fine weather had been settled for some days and the forecast was unusually good. Strictly speaking, any police-man on a function of this nature should be prepared for all types of weather. When he is first notified of his attendance, the order will stipulate: 'Raincoats to be carried'. In reality, not one of us had taken a coat. First mistake of the day.

As our coach throbbed its way through the traffic and up on to the Downs, we saw hundreds of people already picnick-ing from the backs of parked cars. This some five hours before the first race! Direction signs and bill-boards were everywhere: 'Blue Car Park – this way', *'Sporting Life* for the best tips', 'Don't bet till you've consulted MADAM ZARA'.

The race course itself lies almost in the middle of Epsom Downs, which is a plateau of heathland fringed by the stockbroker belt on one side and the toffee-nosed town of Epsom on the other. The course seems almost an intrusion on this rather salubrious area: the elegant Rolls-Royces and distinguished Mercedes look very much in place, but the battered old Vauxhalls and rusty old Fords stand out like spanners in a brassiere.

Our first view of the grandstand was astonishing. We had all complained bitterly when told that we were due to report to the station at 7.30 am.

'That's ridiculous!' we had chorused. 'Who gets to Epsom at nine in the morning?'

Well, we had just found out. Half the world apparently does! There were thousands of people there.

'Whatever time do they arrive?' exclaimed a young PC

from somewhere near the back of the coach. 'The first race isn't till ha' past two!'

'I think they are losers from last year's Derby,' said his companion. 'They've all been too skint to go home!'

The gears of our coach crunched as the driver turned off the road and drove along a short bumpy track into a large fenced-off compound. 'Metropolitan Police. Strictly Private!' read the welcoming sign. Everywhere inside the compound seemed to be a hive of activity, most of it performed by the catering service. Three huge marquees stood in the corner of the area, two of them serving as dining halls and the third as a kitchen. Everywhere was the smell of boiled cabbage. Together with hundreds of my colleagues, I had three meals in the marquees that day and I never once saw cabbage on anyone's plate. Whatever do they do with the stuff?

We all disembarked in our open-necked shirts and instinctively left our tunics on the coach seats. Experience soon tells a constable that if he asks any senior officer on a hot day, 'Should we take our tunics with us?' the answer will always be, 'Yes.' Yet the strange fact is that if no one asks, no one notices.

Inspector Roberts and our two sergeants, Messrs Peter Cage and Jock Livermore, left us to attend a briefing. The rest of us filed into the marquee for a cup of tea. I sat myself next to Tom (Paddy) Ross, a friend of some years' standing. To put Tom on duty at Epsom on Derby Day is akin to locking up a drunk in a brewery. It would never occur to Tom that he is there for any reason other than to 'go racing'. He had spent the whole journey studying form and was only just part of the way through his deliberations. He reluctantly raised his eyes from his *Sporting Life* and made me an offer that I found extremely easy to refuse.

'If you give me twenty quid, you'll leave here in profit. I

*know* I can pick four winners out of the six races.'

'To get twenty quid out of me, Paddy, you'd have to pick six winners out of four races! I've only bet on a horse once in my life and that was Airborne in the 1947 Grand National. I had a shilling on it and I worried for a week. No!'

'But I tell you, you can't go wrong. Look.' He began to spread his papers out all over the canteen table.

'Hullo, Ross! Studying for the promotion exam, are we?' Sergeant Peter Cage had obviously finished at the briefing and he had just entered the marquee.

'Ah, sarge!' exclaimed Tom, with renewed enthusiasm. 'If you give me twenty quid, I'll put you on to some winners.'

'Paddy,' said Peter, emphasizing every word by a slow shake of the head, 'I wouldn't give you twenty quid if you could give me the bloody horse!'

'But – ' began Tom.

'But nothing,' countered Peter. He then looked around at the rest of the group. 'The guv'nor had his briefing and he's got all of your postings for the day. If you'd all like to gather around, he'll tell you what horses you are riding.' He shot a final look at Tom and slowly raised his eyes. 'Twenty quid, tch . . . tch . . .'

Inspector Roberts entered the marquee with a list attached to a clipboard. He began to call out the divisional numbers of those present and then allocated each of them a task. He finally reached the bottom of the list. 'That's about it,' he said. 'Does everyone know exactly what they are supposed to be doing?'

Tom and I exchanged a thoughtful glance – we hadn't been called out. This is always a great dilemma for an experienced constable to find himself in. One thing is for sure: immediately you say, 'You haven't called me out, guv,' then the worst job of the day will come hurtling your way. In this

12

situation it is a good policy for the overlooked party to drag his feet for a couple of minutes. It gives the duty officer sufficient time to say, 'Oh! We haven't posted anyone to the arterial crossroad traffic point, helicopter-pad or gypsy encampment.' I knew this and Tom knew this; unfortunately, there was a fly in the ointment.

'So just what are you two supposed to be doing today, then? No, don't tell me, I know – playboys of the western world?'

Peter Cage then turned his attention from us to the inspector. 'Cole and Ross have been saving themselves for a special job, sir – perhaps traffic point about three miles away from the course?'

'We were going to speak up, weren't we, Tommy?' I protested. 'We just wanted to check first and make sure that we had really been overlooked.'

Disbelief shone from Roberts's eyes as he peered at us over his clipboard. 'W-e-l-l,' he murmured, almost to himself, 'everything seems to be covered. Tell you what. You two can be a mobile reserve for the blokes that we've got down on the crossing place between the winning post and the paddock.'

'What d'you mean, "mobile reserve"?' said Paddy, eyeing the inspector with suspicion.

'Well, you can patrol the area generally, down as far as the paddock. There are only two things for you to remember. Firstly, be on the crossing during every race, particularly being in time for the Queen's walk past, and secondly – ' here he looked directly at Tom – 'I don't want to see *anyone* queuing up in uniform to place a bet. It looks bloody awful. Have a bet by all means, but I don't want to see you do it, understand?'

Paddy nodded, ruefully.

In spite of this slur on his intentions, Tom could not really

13

believe his good fortune. As far as he was concerned, he was in heaven. A roving commission between the paddock and the winning post! What more could anyone ask? It took us twenty minutes to walk down to our positions. Tom used every second of that time to persuade me yet again to assist his attack on the Epsom bookmakers.

'All right, Paddy,' I finally conceded, 'I'll compromise. How about ten quid? All you've got to do then is halve the bet.'

'It doesn't work out like that, and it throws out my calculations. Still, it's better than nothing, I suppose. Don't talk to me for a while, I've got some working-out to do.'

The whole Epsom scene was a totally new concept to me. There must be more nuts and characters on a race course than on any other comparable square mile in the world. Take the tipsters, for example. Many of them look like tramps who have never had a winner in their lives. Yet they are very much the sensible ones. The nuts are the punters who queue to buy tips from them. Then there are the fortune-tellers. We must have passed twenty caravans on our stroll down to the paddock, each of them claiming to house 'The Original Gypsy Lee', 'Madame Zoro' or 'Princess Zena'. Most of them exhibited huge faded photographs of their huge faded owners. In many of these photographs the fortune-tellers shared a pose with a show-business nonentity of some two decades past. Several of these ladies called out to us as we passed, 'Come on young sirs' (Tom and I shared ninety-two years between us!), 'let me read your palm. I'll ensure you luck and romance.' Forget the romance, I thought, I would be quite happy to get my ten quid back.

The sun had now climbed very high and so had the temperature: eighty-four Fahrenheit, to be precise. There was still some two and a half hours to go before the first race but already thousands of people thronged the course. Tom had at last worked out his formula for the day. I never understood a word of it, but he had apparently picked out six winners and we needed a horse called Brondesbury to win the first race. We also needed Golden Fleece to win the Derby itself but after that, he assured me, it was going to be downhill all the way.

Alongside the paddock at Epsom, slightly away from the race course proper, is the tote, and it was there that Tom decided to place our bets.

'Okay, you keep an eye out for the guv'nor and I'll win us some money.' Carrying numerous papers and slips, he walked thoughtfully towards a small window.

I stood some fifteen yards back from the tote, propping myself up against a rail. I remember thinking what a brass neck he had. Suddenly, two women aged about thirty, deep in conversation, walked past me. They made for a staircase that led up to a bar on the floor above the tote. This was not in itself peculiar: the bar was now open and customers had been entering from time to time. What was unusual, however, was that on a day which abounded with beautiful women, these two were probably the best. A rare double bonus.

I instantly forgot Tom as I watched both ladies shimmer in their gossamer-like dresses towards the staircase. When they reached the first step, the darker of the two slipped her hand casually into the palm of the other's. I thought little of this until they had completely climbed the first flight. They were now out of sight of everyone — everyone, that is, except me. Suddenly the fairer of the two wheeled on her beautiful companion; she then threw her arms around her neck and kissed her passionately! Her partner reacted by momentarily locking the fair one in an embrace that was equally responsive.

The embracer then proceeded to caress her friend's body in a way that almost caused me to fall from my rail. The whole encounter was over in about thirty seconds, but it left me stunned. I had never seen anything so instantly erotic in my life! The two women then stepped back from their embrace and quickly smoothed down their dresses – this time their own. They then continued around the corner and, presumably, up the stairs, just as if nothing had happened.

I messily gathered my wits together. I swung my vision around to the right and was about to call Tom away from the tote window. I already had the words 'Did you see that?' shaped in my mouth. One problem with middle age is that it always takes my eyes a full second to refocus. As the helmeted blur reshaped itself into Paddy's features, I realized that he was no longer crouched intently over a small window sill. In fact he was standing there gaping away to my left. He still had his bets in his hand, and wore a decidedly silly expression on his face. I followed his line of vision and there, purposefully striding towards me, was a chief superintendent and an accompanying sergeant, neither of whom I had ever seen before. They walked straight past me for just a few yards and then stopped at an equal distance between Paddy and myself. Tom cleared his throat. He thought he was obviously expected to say something. I was totally intrigued as to just what it would be. I had heard of 'bang to rights' but this was ridiculous. Before the first words could leave Tom's lips, the chief superintendent spoke.

'Well, go on, then,' he said to Tom. 'If you miss a winner because of me, you'll be convinced that I am the biggest shit in the whole world. But I tell you something,' he paused and looked around to me. He then returned his gaze to the speechless Tom. 'I don't think a lot of your look-out!' Then, with his eyes twinkling and his sergeant desperately trying to hide a smile, he strode away.

Paddy scuttled quickly back to the window before launching into his expected verbal attack on me. I started to explain about the two off-beat beauties but he was in no mood for excuses.

'C'mon, then, I'll buy you a drink,' I said. The saying of that by any policeman constitutes a complete admission of guilt.

We followed the trail of the two ladies up the staircase and along to the several bars. These were well patronized and therefore presented us with a problem. If it were frowned upon to place a bet in uniform, to be discovered queuing up for a pint would be a capital offence.

'How about there?' said Paddy, pointing to a large room that was stacked high with crates.

Inside, a solitary peroxide blonde was wiping over a counter top. As we entered the room, the blonde looked up and instantly showed years of experience.

'I suppose you two layabouts 'ave crept in for a drink?'

'Well, er, yes, the other bars were a little crowded,' I faltered.

'That's all right. I was just abaht ter 'ave one meself. You can join me if yer like. I puts 'em dahn ter breakages,' she said, with a knowing wink. She was not the most wholesome character that I had ever seen but her heart seemed to be in the right place. 'Bottles are a bit dirty, luv. Still, neve' mind, eh? I'll give 'em a bit of a wipe over.'

With that she dived down into her handbag and took out quite the filthiest handkerchief that I had ever seen. Paddy's nose had a definite wrinkle, although it did not seem to stop him drinking her beer. We bravely finished our drinks and took a smart leave of our chatty hostess, gallantly declining her offer of renewed hospitality.

We walked out on to the balcony that led to the staircase.

If anything, the temperature had become even hotter while we were inside. I wiped the perspiration from the sweatband of my helmet. We paused momentarily to take in the scene on the ground just beneath us. It was certainly the day of the very beautiful people, ninety-nine per cent of whom also happened to be very rich. It was a whole different world down there. I began to amuse myself with a face-spotting competition.

'You know who I'd like to see?' Tom asked me wistfully. 'Maybe even speak to,' he added reverently. I ran quickly through my most obvious recollections of film stars, show-biz personalities, world leaders and strippers. It was none of them. 'All right, I give in. Just who is it that you want to see more than anyone else?'

'Wee Jerry.'

'Who?'

'Wee Jerry!'

'Well who the bloody hell is "Wee Jerry"?'

'Wee Jerry? He's the head lad of Golden Fleece. That just happens to be the horse that you've bet on in the Derby!'

'What d'you mean, "the horse that *I've* bet on"? I thought we had *split* all of the bets!'

'Well, *I've* not bet on it. I wanted to be sure first. That's why I would like to see the head lad.'

'Cor, you're bloody priceless, you are! You blag me for ten quid to put on some stupid horses and it turns out that you've not even bet on 'em yourself! You must be the Ulster branch of the Mafia!'

'Listen,' he said patiently (and Tommy is *not* a patient man), 'I happen to think that Golden Fleece is going to win the Derby. All I'm asking is a chance to confirm it with his head lad. What's wrong with that?'

'What's wrong with that?!! There'll be close on half a

million people here today, that's what's wrong with that! Are they all going to form a sodding queue to ask your bloody Jerry whether or not his stupid horse is going to win the Derby! You've got some front, you have!'

'Well, I think you're making far too big a thing of this,' murmured Tom in a wounded manner, 'and besides, here comes Roberts and Peter Cage.'

Our argument . had caused our vigilance to slip, and Roberts had seen us even before we had seen him. There was therefore little point in dashing down to ground level. We held our ground and looked suitably conscientious as the two of them climbed to the top of the stairs. Peter Cage was the first of them to draw breath.

'Airs of grandeur, have we, Cole? Hob-nobbing with the gentry, Ross? You want to be careful, they're probably the ones that burnt down your shack and turned it over to sheep.'

'Looking for pickpockets, sergeant. Quite a good view of the paddock from up here. We can see everything,' I responded – rather neatly, I thought.

'Well, not quite everything,' said Roberts. 'You didn't see us, for a start.'

'Just goes to prove that our consciences are clean, sir – we had no reason to be looking for you,' stated Tom, smugly.

All in all I thought we had won.

Roberts obviously thought so too because he nodded in seeming admiration. 'Don't forget the Queen. Be in position at three o'clock. I'll see you both then.'

I instinctively looked at Peter Cage for his parting shot. 'You will let Her Majesty know if you can't make it, though, won't you?' I wasn't disappointed.

Tom and I followed them both down the stairs. Every few yards I craned my neck in a vain effort to see my two ladies.

19

This frustrating searching was finally getting through to Tom. 'C'mon,' he said, irritably, 'let's have a walk around the tents.'

Now the word 'tents' was a crass understatement. On two sides of the paddock on Derby Day, palatial reception rooms are erected. In these rooms, extremely expensive clients, of extremely expensive businesses, are entertained to extremely expensive lunches. There are hostesses, waiters and plush red carpets.

'Look at this lot,' said Paddy. 'And you are worrying about your ten-quid bet! God but you're small-minded!'

'But these aren't tents! Tents are what boy scouts and brownies put up in the rain. You'd have to be at least a duke or a marchioness here to be allowed past the guy ropes!'

There was only one more tent for us to admire, a much less grand affair nestling under a great beech tree. It was of oblong shape with a very attractive young lady seated just inside the wide entrance. All around the walls of the tent were paintings, mostly of racing scenes, and small carvings. The sign outside read 'Kensington Arts'. Tom had decided he needed a cigarette. He therefore began to pass the time of day with the tent's only occupant. This was no selection of pure chance. Kensington Arts looked like the only company that might be tolerant enough to allow us in! I left Tommy to do the talking – it is something that he is quite proficient at – and interested myself in the paintings. I was vaguely aware that the two of them were discussing the big race, but I was already bored to tears with racing talk. Suddenly a spoken sentence cut through my indifference.

'O' course, what I'd really like is to see Wee Jerry.'

'Oh, hell, no!' I thought, 'we are not going through all of that "Wee Jerry" bit again, surely.'

'Well,' said the girl, 'all you have to do is to look behind you – he's just coming in the tent!'

We both wheeled around. There, striding through the doorway, was a friendly faced little Irishman with a ready smile and twinkling eyes. Wee Jerry himself!!

'Bloody hell, mate!' I burst out. 'You're better than Aladdin. You must have come out of a hole in the ground.'

If Tom thought that he was in heaven simply by being at Epsom, then he was convinced he had now met the Messiah.

The worst part of the whole day for me was when Tommy and Jerry discovered that they came from the same village! There can be few things more boring in the world than two Irishmen reminiscing about their childhood. Their conversation was finally terminated by the distant sound of thunder. I looked out of the tent but the sky seemed totally blue, with not as much as a breath of air about. However, in the far south-west and many miles away across the Downs could be seen just a few black clouds. They were so still that they appeared to have been painted on the sky.

'Oh, I don't think that it'll come this way,' I said confidently. 'It's absolutely miles away and nothing is moving in the atmosphere at all.' My casual use of the word 'atmosphere' immediately convinced several people who were looking anxiously up at the sky that I knew what I was talking about. They were very reassured.

Tom and Jerry were parting about as reluctantly as did their counterparts Romeo and Juliet.

'C'mon, Paddy,' I said impatiently. 'We've got to eat before the racing begins.'

'Okay. One last thing, Jerry. How will the race go?'

'If Golden Fleece is third or fourth at Tattenham corner, then he'll be a winner,' said the head lad with all the confidence in the world.

My own confidence actually faded at this stage. The thought of my ten quid riding on a nag that was expected to have three competitors in front of it with only two furlongs to go, was just about the final straw.

I spent a frustrating thirty minutes at lunch trying to get Tom to talk to me. But my attempts at conversation were answered by nothing but grunts. It was like being married to him. He barely raised his head as he pored over race-cards, newspapers and form-guides.

'Right, I've got it!' he suddenly exclaimed.

'Got what?'

'The card – I've gone through the card and I have a winner for every race. We'll clear up hundreds today, you see if we don't!'

'Will I get my ten quid back?'

'C'mon,' he said, ignoring my question, 'I've got to get on Brondesbury in the first race at two o'clock.'

'But I thought we had already bet on that horse?'

'No! All I did was bet on it with your money. Now I'm using mine!'

'That's supposed to make me feel better?'

We left the remains of our cabbageless lunch and dutifully made our way back to our designated patrol. The thunder was by now alarmingly frequent, and huge coppery-edged black clouds assembled just away to our west. We stopped at the tote only long enough for Tom to place his rather complicated bets. A particularly loud crash of thunder suddenly exploded all around us. It ricocheted from the beech tree to the tote and back to the tree again. As we rapidly sought shelter in the Kensington Arts tent, the first of the great wet splodges smacked against our summer shirts. Within seconds the heavy, still air had been transformed into some rain-forest deluge.

Top-hatted gentlemen and their delicately expensive ladies cast dignity aside as they scuttled for any available cover. The small friendly tent now housed some thirty greatly relieved people. Anyone who had failed to obtain shelter within the first minute was now soaked beyond salvation and likely to remain so. While the rain reduced the temperature a little, it still remained well into the eighties.

Some thirty minutes later, the storm ended as instantly as it had begun. It had been like some great amphibious prelude. Its timing had been so precise that I considered checking Tom's race-card to see if it had been part of the official programme.

We emerged from our tent as the sun emerged from the cloud. We blinked a greeting and hurried away to our crossing-point. The sight that met our eyes was truly astonishing. The whole of Epsom Downs looked like some gigantic nipple convention. Every soaked female was virtually naked! There were some three hundred thousand people at the Derby and there was cover for just some five per cent of them. The remainder were not simply wet, they were totally saturated. Every light-coloured dress, blouse or shirt was now completely transparent! And this included the WPCs. In fact our own girl, Celia, reckoned that half of the force already had eye trouble.

'What sort of eye trouble?' I asked, naively.

'It's the sort where their eyes won't go back into their heads,' she explained.

'Ah, yes,' I acknowledged, trying desperately hard to look her in the face.

'They are under starter's orders. They're off!' boomed the voice of the commentator over the loud-speakers.

The pedestrian crossing-point had now been closed for some minutes and we craned our heads to see down the course. Suddenly the first of the horses sped around Tat-tenham corner.

'It's him, he's going well,' exclaimed Tom, emotionally.

They ran in a confused bunch up the hill and past the stand.

'And at the post it's Brondesbury first ...' came the metallic voice once again.

'That's our horse, Paddy, that's our bloody horse! C'mon, who've we got in the next race?'

The spectator crossing was now thrown open and I assumed there was little for Tommy and I to do except collect our winnings. But betting with Tom is not as simple as that.

'No, no, no,' he explained. 'I've worked it all out from every angle. We have trebles, cross-doubles, accumulators and yankees.'

'Do you mean that although my horse has romped home a winner, I have no money to come?'

'That's right. It's all going on to Buffavento and Golden Brigadier in the two thirty-five.'

'But supposing neither of them wins?'

'Don't worry, one of them will. And anyway, if they don't we'll just start again with Golden Fleece in the Derby.'

'Oh, you mean the horse that needs to be fourth, just when I think that he ought to be winning?'

'Oh don't be so bloody miserable! C'mon, let's go to the paddock. We can have a good look at Buffavento before he races.'

I tagged behind him like some sulking child.

A few minutes later we entered the paddock – or at least Paddy did – just as the horses for the two thirty-five were being led around. He studied every horse with the intensity of an obsessed vet. I never actually set foot in the paddock

24

proper. I just stood in the gangway and stared idly at the spectators.

My attention was soon taken by a very good-looking couple. He was of excellent physique and very smart appearance, while she appeared to be just absolutely beautiful. I say 'appeared' because no matter how I adjusted my position, I could never quite see her face. A broad hand-rail obscured her features as efficiently as any yashmak. She sat casually draped across several paddock steps, her demeanour suggesting that she felt as indifferent to horse-racing as I was. Because I found her far more interesting than any horse, I gradually began to take a careful stock.

First, she looked expensive. Absolutely everything about her oozed Harrods. She wore a pure white silk suit, with a very low-cut, royal blue blouse. A small but superbly styled hat rested on her head at a seductive angle. At the other end, her high-heeled sandals definitely did not originate from Dolcis. In between these two extremes was a suntan that looked as extravagant as her outfit. A delicate bracelet, only slightly less golden than her skin, hung from her right wrist, while her left wrist housed a watch of a most unusual design.

As I watched her, her left hand rose casually and brushed some troublesome insect from the swell of her left breast. The wrist-watch momentarily caught the glare of the sun and bounced its rays straight back into my eyes. Once the fierce glare had faded, I was left with a fixed mental picture of an arm, a watch and a breast, all matching in colour and symmetrically perfect. I ducked my head to see underneath the rail, and at that precise moment she turned her body away to speak to her escort who was standing nonchalantly behind her. They conversed for some minutes, then he took both her hands and pulled her to her feet. They walked then towards the far exit, leaving me hypnotized by the rhythmical swing of her skirt.

'Wassamatter with you?' said Tom's distant voice.

'Uh? Oh, Paddy, I'm in love! I've just seen the most beautiful creature in the world, at least I think that I have. Whatever we do today, Paddy, we have got to see that girl's face!'

'She's probably got a Hitler moustache and Dunlopillo lips! C'mon, I want to see Buffavento go up to the start.'

I sighed and, for the umpteenth time that day, followed meekly behind.

For someone who is as uninitiated into the racing world as I am, the speed at which the horses gallop up to the start is astonishing. We returned to our colleagues on the crossing and waited for the voice of the announcer. Buffavento never received as much as a mention. As for Golden Brigadier, I think that he must have fallen dead somewhere on the far side of the Down.

'What now?' I asked, almost tearfully.

'Start again. Don't worry, Wee Jerry'll do it!'

Around three o'clock, the royal party usually walk along a section of the course between the grandstand and the paddock. Then, in the ring, they watch the parade of the Derby horses. Apart from attending to the crossing between each race, this royal stroll was to be our only duty obligation that day. There was, however, some speculation that this walk might have to be cancelled because the grass on the course, which was rather long, was still extremely wet from the storm. It was for this reason that the Queen's car drove unexpectedly on to the course and met the royal party at the foot of the grandstand steps.

Incredible though it may seem, there are a great number of

people who arrive early to secure a position on the rails for no other reason than to see the Queen. A rather pleasant mum with two small children was just such a person. She leaned forward from her position behind the rails and asked me what was happening. I pointed out the problem with the wet grass.

'Oh, no!' she cried. 'We've only come for the Queen. The kids will be so disappointed.'

From my position in front of the rails, I saw the Queen wave her car away and begin to lead her party down the course on foot. The driver then began a 'U' turn and headed slowly back in our direction.

'What's your name, luv?' I asked her.

'My name? Well, it's Doreen, why?'

'Well, I'm going to have a quick word with my guv'nor there.' I pointed to Inspector Roberts some fifteen yards away and slightly out of her view. 'I'll get him to tell the Queen on the radio that you have come here today just to see her. After all, if you have made an effort to see her, I think that it is only right and proper that she should make an effort to see you.'

I then moved quickly out of her vision. After some thirty seconds and just before the main royal party came into her view, I returned.

'Yes, that's quite okay, luv. Apparently she said, "For Doreen, anything!" '

Doreen eyed me suspiciously. 'You lying sod,' she uttered, quietly.

In spite of her words, I could see that she was very unsure. 'Would I lie to you, luv? Look over there — who's that walking down the course, then?' I pointed to the Queen chatting merrily to a top-hatted gentleman wearing the worst fitting suit that I had ever seen.

Doreen gasped, and scrambled for her Polaroid. 'I still don't believe you – but thanks!'

' 'Ere, just a minute!'

I turned to see a bearded, aggressive-looking fellow standing just behind Doreen and her children.

'Yes, mate?' I answered as politely as I could, having no wish to upset anyone who looked so belligerent.

'Wasn't the Queen in that car?'

'No!'

'Well, who was, then?'

'Nobody was.'

'Then I've taken a picture of an empty car?'

'Well, yes, if that's what you've done, I suppose you have!'

'That's your bloody fault,' he snapped, wheeling on Doreen. 'That was the last picture on my roll. And you're as much to blame as he is!'

With that, he forced his way out of the crowd and disappeared over the heath.

'You're a right trouble-maker, you are, Doreen. When're you going home?' I asked.

I was aware of Tom sidling up to me. 'Hey,' he said, 'let's slip down to the paddock, I want to see Golden Fleece.'

'Leave it out, Paddy, that'd look just great, wouldn't it? You, me and the Queen, all carefully studying the Derby prospects! Anyway, you'll see them soon enough as they canter up to the start.'

'It's not the same,' he pouted.

Some fifteen minutes later, the Queen and her party returned to the grandstand. The chief superintendent, together with his sergeant whom we had encountered earlier, formed part of her escort. On seeing us standing so smartly to attention, he acknowledged with a nod.

The horses shortly followed on their way to the one-and-a-half-mile start. A buzz of expectancy now arose from the crowd and built up into an almost continual roar. The announcer's voice again cut dramatically through everyone's conversation.

'They're under starter's orders . . . They're off!'

An explosion of yells, shrieks and horses' names emitted from almost every throat on the Downs. The pigeons and sparrows perching expectantly on roofs and trees fluttered up in alarm.

From our position on the course we would see very little until the horses emerged around Tattenham corner. We therefore relied totally on the commentary. The speaker fired out a jumble of names and just occasionally that of Golden Fleece. Suddenly, the horses burst around Tattenham corner. Away in the distance I heard the sentence, 'Golden Fleece is lying fourth.' Had not Wee Jerry said that? No, surely races are not won by a horse lying fourth? Or are they? As they came up the hill, so the name Golden Fleece was repeated more and more.

'And at the post it's Golden Fleece!'

I was beginning to think that perhaps Paddy was a genius, after all.

While we remained in position and waited for the crossing to reopen, I suddenly saw a happy, smiling little leprechaun of a man skipping happily towards the unsaddling enclosure. Wee Jerry was over the moon! Soon the word came to reopen the crossing and Paddy and I quickly raced down to the tote.

'Three-to-one,' he chirruped, 'not bad for the favourite. That's put us back into the black again.'

I suddenly came face to face with the chief superintendent and his sergeant.

'Well, did you do the winner?' he asked.

'Yes, guv,' I answered, just as casually as I could, hoping that he would not realize I did not know the first thing about racing.

'Are you showing a profit so far?'

'Yes, yes. We're really quite well ahead now,' I bleated. I was wondering if I should throw in some vague horse-racing expression that I had heard somewhere or other.

'Oh, well, off you go,' he commanded, 'and pick up your winnings, but not too obviously!'

As the pair of them strode away, I wheeled angrily on Paddy. 'Why didn't you help me out there? You know full well that I know absolutely nothing about racing. He must have thought that I was a right burke!'

'I never like talking to senior officers when I am betting on horses,' he answered.

'Oh yes,' I snapped, 'I had almost forgotten that. They are still your bloody bets, aren't they? I don't clean up until the end of the day, do I?'

'You're doing very . . .'

'Hey, Paddy!' I interrupted. 'Look, it's her! That woman, the one from the paddock! Jeepers, she's absolutely beautiful! I knew it! I just knew she would be!'

Some twenty yards ahead, and making straight towards us, was the couple from the paddock. 'I wonder if you two gentlemen could help us,' said her escort. 'We appear to have been robbed.'

'Robbed! What, here in the paddock?' asked Tommy incredulously.

'Well, perhaps not robbed, then. I have no idea what your technical term is for it. But this young lady has lost her watch. It simply must have been stolen. It was very well secured on her wrist. It was also very expensive!' he added, darkly.

I stared dewy-eyed at her. 'You had it on about one and a half hours ago,' I murmured.

'How on earth do you know that?' she said – actually speaking to me!

'Because I saw it. It had rather an unusual shape. It had a widish face that tapered narrowly into a thin band.'

'Good God, man, that's positively amazing!' said the escort. 'There are hundreds of thousands of people here today. How can you possibly remember anything so detailed as a wrist-watch?'

Seizing my opportunity, I then decided to be really impressive. 'She was wearing that watch at exactly twenty past two. She was in fact wearing it when you pulled her up from a sitting position and walked out of that far exit.' I pointed grandly towards the corner of the paddock.

'Well, I've never known anything like it!' he exclaimed. 'You must have a photographic memory!'

Tom made what was probably a timely interruption. I would certainly have committed an overkill if I had been permitted to carry on much longer.

'Yes, I'll tell you what, guv,' he suggested. 'You go down to the police office at the back of the stand and report the loss officially there. Meanwhile we will carry on here looking for the lady's watch. After all,' he shot a meaningful glance at me, 'we do know exactly what it looks like, don't we?'

'Yes, that's an excellent idea. Yes, thank you very much. Come on, Maude, we'll do that, it may have been handed in. Let's hurry!'

Maude! Oh, no! That can't be her name. I wouldn't have taken her for a Maude in a million years. Desirée, yes! Or perhaps even Yolande, but Maude? Never!

As they hurried away, I could hear the adjectives tumbling into the distance. 'Incredible', 'Superb', 'Amazing'.

31

'Bull-shit!' blasted Paddy.

I refused to be drawn by his jealousy. 'You've got to admit it, Paddy. I was masterly, and she was lovely. Yes?'

'C'mon,' he growled. 'I've got ten quid at three-to-one.'

'You go and get your winnings. I'll go to the paddock and look for the watch.' I sighed deeply. 'You never know, I might find it. Maude might then wish to show her eternal gratitude by . . .' I looked around, I was talking to myself. He had gone.

I began to assess the day so far. It was really going very well. We were in profit with just three races to go. It had just turned four o'clock and we were now on overtime. The thought of winning money from bookmakers at overtime rate made me feel exceedingly good. It is true that I had not found the watch, but Tom was fast approaching with the news of our next two horses: Johnny Nobody in the four twenty and Tender King in the four fifty. These mounts would pave the way for our final killing on Lord Wimpy in the five twenty-five. Unfortunately, while we were happily returning to our crossing, Johnny Nobody proved exactly why he was so-called. Tender King then disappeared somewhere, presumably looking for Golden Brigadier. The magic was fading fast.

'Lord Wimpy will get us out of trouble,' said Paddy confidently. 'We'll put a few quid on this last race and we'll do really well. Want to put a tenner on?'

'No, I don't! What's the matter with the tenner that I've already given you?'

'Oh, don't worry about that, that's perfectly all right. It's just that another tenner on Lord Wimpy will ensure a very good day indeed.'

'No!'

This time Tom did not go to the tote. He took me on a hike

all across the Downs in an effort to find the best odds. We must have studied twenty bookies' boards before he finally found one that satisfied him.

'I've got fives,' he said, proudly. 'Not bad, eh? Not bad at all. All we want now is for the thing to win!'

As we headed back to our crossing, we yet again came face to face with the chief superintendent and his sergeant. 'You'd think with all of these people here we'd be able to give him the slip, wouldn't you?' I moaned.

'Hullo, lads, don't tell me – you're doing a getting-out-of-trouble bet. Yes?'

'Yes,' agreed Paddy, rather dejectedly, I felt.

'Who've you done?'

'Lord Wimpy, guv.'

'Sensible choice, can't lose,' he agreed.

Oh bloody hell, I thought, not another one!

The race itself was something of an anti-climax. Lord Wimpy led from start to finish. He simply towed the other mounts home. The crowd was by now drifting away fast as we threaded our way first to Tom's bookmaker and then to the tote. When we were just a few yards from the tote window, the chief superintendent and his seemingly permanent shadow appeared for the last time.

'Have you had a good day, lads?'

'Yessir!' we chorused.

'Have you enjoyed yourselves?' he persisted.

'Oh yes, sir, very much!'

'Are either of you on duty here tomorrow?'

'No, sir!'

'Thank God!' he exclaimed, putting his hands together and walking slowly on past us.

After a few minutes' queuing at the window Tom returned, busily checking our finances.

'Are we going to, er, settle up, Paddy?' I asked with a false air of indifference.

'Settle up? Oh, yes. I won thirty quid over all,' he said, proudly.

'Yes, but how did I do?'

'You? Oh, you lost two quid.'

'What do you mean, I lost two quid? How can I lose two quid – you won thirty and we both bet on the same horses?'

'Easy – I had more money on the winners than you did. See?'

No, I didn't see at all, but I was battle-weary and wanted to go home. I had eight pounds back, which was eight pounds more than I had expected.

The whole Walworth Road contingent assembled at the crossing. We swapped stories of the day's events and still the sun beat mercilessly down. Celia had by this time completely dried out, so we could at least quite freely converse again. Just alongside our crossing was a telephone box. It appeared to be the only one in that part of the Downs. A great queue of people stretched some distance away from its door. It suddenly occurred to us that the queue was caused not so much by the volume of callers as by the reluctance of one particular caller to leave the box.

Twenty-five minutes had elapsed and several members of the queue were becoming very agitated. It was difficult for us to ignore this fact because the entire twenty-three of us were standing within fifteen yards of the box. Finally, two young girls near the head of the line asked one of our group for his assistance. The PC put his head in the box and quite politely asked the occupier to speed things up a little. The result was astonishing. He leapt from the box clutching a can of Foster's lager. He then proceeded to claim an infringement of his civil rights.

'Just who do you think you are? I've got a lot of time for you fellows as a rule, I'm always on your side, but never again!' I had already decided that he was the one person in the world whom I did not want on my side. 'You have absolutely no right to speak to me in a phone box,' he continued. 'I want your number, I'm going to report you!'

'Look, go home, there's a good fellah,' said the constable, wearily.

If anything, this seemed to inflame him more than ever. 'Right, that's it! What's your number?'

The PC turned his shoulder slightly towards him, thereby displaying his number, but wisely said nothing. The way the situation was developing, it seemed certain that sooner or later someone would be nicking him. This would not be good news, because we could then be delayed in getting away. I am normally fairly restrained in these circumstances, but for some reason he was really getting through to me.

'Did you hear me?' he persisted. 'I want your number!'

I was the first to crack. 'Oy! What's the matter with you?' I snapped.

'This is nothing to do with you. I want a pencil to take down this man's number. He's been rude to me!'

'Well, in that case you had better get prepared to take my number as well, because you are without doubt the greatest pain-in-the-arse that I've met today. You are selfish, inconsiderate and a pompous half-drunk bore! You are also extremely lucky! So go home.'

'Right! I want your number as well. Give me a pencil!'

'If you want to make a complaint, mate, you can buy your own pencil. Now hop it, and don't annoy the constables. We've been on our feet all day and we are extremely tired.'

'He's also lost two quid,' said Tommy, unhelpfully.

The call came over our radio that we were to return to the

35

coach. We left our complainant trying to recite six police numbers parrot-fashion. Each time he got them wrong.

As we threaded our way across the heath there were hundreds of coaches all parked in lines. Traffic on the main roads was barely moving, so most of the occupants were sensibly seeing out the early evening with ball-games and booze. All the coaches had their boots open, and beer was being liberally served from most of them. Old cockney ladies sang old cockney songs in great flowered hats – they paused only to kiss the youngest of the policemen!

The journey home took over two hours but I slept for most of it.

'You know what I've been thinking?' said Paddy as we drove down the Walworth Road.

'No – what?' I answered, with total disinterest.

'I thought that next year we could organize a proper station outing to the Derby. Don't you think that's a good idea?'

## Vote, Vote, Vote

The small talk of twenty-two parading policemen is no different from that of any comparable body. All the usual subjects were aired that afternoon as we waited in the station parade room for our election-day duties.

'Have you seen Trevor's new bike? It's a monster! He's just got done for speeding by the Kent police. One hundred and twenty mph on the motorway!'

'Have you seen the legs on the new WPC?'

'I hear that she wears stockings and suspenders instead of tights!'

'Wow.'

'Will he lose his job?'

'Imagine those thighs in suspenders!'

'Whose, Trevor's?'

'No, you burke, Cynthia's.'

'Hey, I heard about that Cynthia, they reckon . . .'

'Right, pay attention, you lot! Here are your election-day duties.' I felt quite put out as the arrival of Sergeant Cage interrupted some fascinating revelation about the statuesque Cynthia.

I do not usually share in this pre-parade small talk. The hours normally worked by a community copper do not coincide with those of the regular shifts. It only did so today because of the by-election. Each polling station would be covered by a policeman, who would be responsible to the section sergeant. This would be my last election before I left the force. I had been covering them, both parliamentary and local, for thirty years. I would quite miss them because I had always found them to be great fun.

'Oh ho! It's Constable Cole! Say hullo to Constable Cole, everyone. This is indeed a privilege.' Peter Cage bowed deferentially and slipped immediately into his antagonize-Harry-Cole routine. 'To what do we owe the honour?'

'Guv'nor thought it would be a good idea to have a little experience and subtlety in the day, sarge. All of these young men –' I pointed up and down the two rows, 'are doubtless very good but you can't beat experience and subtlety.'

'Experience and subtlety – so that's what it is! Is that what you've been suffering from all of these years? I see,' he nodded, thoughtfully. 'God only knows what you're experienced in. I've never seen you do anything. But subtlety? Well, that's something else.' He peered at me over his clipboard for a few seconds. 'D'you know, I think you're about as subtle as a hundredweight of prunes?'

'Are all of the men posted, sergeant?' asked Inspector Fellows as he strode purposefully into the room.

'Not yet, sir, Constable Cole has just had quite a nasty turn. He thinks he's got "subtlety". I think it's more likely to be something to do with his bowels.'

'Well, post him to the polling station nearest to the nick, just in case it is. D'you mind if we get on now?' Fellows looked somewhat impatiently towards me.

'It's nothing to do with me, sir, it's him.' I indignantly pointed at Peter. 'He's always having a go at me!'

Peter was scribbling away intently on his clipboard. He did not look up but muttered almost to himself as he wrote, 'Experience, subtlety, persecution mania . . .'

True to Fellows's suggestion, I had been given one of the

polling stations closest to Wharf Road. This had little to do with any condition that I may have, either real or imaginary. It was simply that St Mark's School was roughly in the centre of my regular patch. I picked up a library book and some sandwiches and six minutes later I entered the school.

A local villain once told me that he could always recognize nurses and policemen out of uniform. 'They are all the same type,' he claimed. Well, I am not sure of the accuracy of that observation, but unquestionably the people who staff polling stations are all chipped out of the same mould. There are two things you can rely on: they will feel the cold badly, and will drink tea incessantly. The three who were working at my station that day could have been the son and daughters of the three who formed my first panel, some thirty years ago. Absolutely nothing changes. The desk that they sit behind is even cluttered up with the same paraphernalia. Five daily papers, two library books, three dirty teacups, an unclipped handbag, an opened packet of cigarettes, two packets of biscuits, one bag of sweets and a partially eaten apple.

The two young ladies were pleasantly attractive, and the man, who was also the presiding officer in charge, seemed both friendly and competent. I introduced myself as their late-turn policeman and they welcomed me with the customary mug of tea. After a day's duty at a polling station, the average copper will usually slurp back to his police station, tea coming out of his ears.

The presiding officer, usually the most senior of the three staff, has almost absolute power in the running of the polling station, although obviously he is strictly governed by the Representation of the People Act. Policemen are always instructed to accede to his every whim. I never met a presiding officer who abused this privilege.

Having downed my first cup of tea of the day, I began to

be aware of just how uncomfortably hot the place was. I moved across the room and stood in a draught, there it was only *just* hot. Everywhere else you could grow rubber. The staff seemed somehow unaware of this. The double cardigan of one of the girls was, I suppose, partially offset by a huge hole in the elbow. But other than this hole, they all appeared dressed for Alaska.

I decided to stand at the door for a while. The afternoon was pleasant and it would be nice to enjoy the last of the day's sunshine. It was while standing at the door that I noticed Tim McShutey wandering around at the rear of the playground. I had known Tim for some years. He was a pleasant, red-faced Irishman, usually drunk but always ultra-friendly. His great problem, apart, of course, from his drinking, was his eldest son Benny. Benny had developed into a mean little pickpocket and was unfortunately very good at his trade. Tim did not approve of this vocation but Benny was a vicious young man and held sway over the objections of his father. Tim had one other problem: drunk or sober, he was *not* very bright.

'What on earth are you doing over there, Tim?' I called.

He turned and noticed me for the first time. His round red face broke into a great smile. 'Hullo, Mr Cole, sur, Oi'm trying to vote, sur!'

'But what're you doing right over there?'

'Oi karn't foind der place, sur!'

'But you must have walked straight past it! It's here, where the big notice says "Polling Station".' I pointed at the sign – it was one of six, all about four feet long. They each spelt out POLLING STATION in large black and white capitals.

'Oi didern't know dat, sur. Oi'll vote now, sur.' He walked across the playground and pumped my hand in an honest

40

gesture of friendship. 'Who d'yer think'll get in, sur? I tink Maggie'll get in, meself.'

'Maggie? But she's not standing. There's only one election today and that's here in this borough. It's not all over the country, you know.'

'It's not, sur? Oh, Oi see, sur.' He thought for a moment, then again looked up at me. 'So Oi karn't vote for Maggie, den, sur?'

'Well, yes, you can vote for her candidate. But you can't actually vote for Mrs Thatcher herself, no.'

'Dat's quite differcult, den, sur, isn't it?'

'No, you just put a cross on the form alongside the Conservative candidate.'

'You aren't allowed to say that!' exclaimed a voice from close by. I looked around and saw the Labour Party supporter who was sitting at the door collecting the voters' old polling cards as they left the station. 'You can't tell him who to vote for while you are on duty!' he persisted.

'I'm not telling him who to vote for, I don't give a sod who he votes for! He said he wanted to vote for Thatcher and I told him that if he wanted to do that, then he must vote for the Conservative Party candidate, that's all. I'd have told him the equivalent thing if he'd said that he wanted Michael Foot!'

'Don't get me wrong,' said the Labour man. 'I appreciate your intentions. You just shouldn't have tried to influence his vote, that's all. It's an infringement of the Representation of the People Act.'

For a policeman, the Representation of the People Act is always a pain in the neck. The average copper has no more than a cursory knowledge of it anyway. The trouble is that on election days everyone else is an expert – or at least they claim to be. The question that a policeman then has to ask

41

himself is just how much do they know. How far can they be bluffed? I was about to find out. I took a deep breath and began: 'The Representation of the People Act clearly defines that although visual aids are not allowed within the precincts of any polling station, verbal advice *can* be given – *when sought* – right up until the time that the candidate casts his vote. The operative phrase here, of course, is "when sought" – agreed?'

To my pleasant surprise, the reply came back, 'Oh, of course, you're quite right, I remember now.'

You bloody liar, I thought, you know less about the Representation of the People Act than I do! After that, we got on famously. With the assistance of the Labour man, Tim finally found his way into the building.

The atmosphere between the three card-collectors at the door was really quite good. Only the three main parties were represented, Labour, Conservative and the Social Democrats. The smaller parties did not have sufficient support or finances. Every half an hour or so, couriers would arrive from the three party headquarters and carry away any cards that their collectors had amassed. On many of these regular calls, the courier finds there are no cards at all!

At every election that I have ever policed, I have asked at least one collector the main purpose of this system. None has been able to tell me. I think it is a throwback to the days of high electorate turnout.

Some ten minutes later, Tim emerged from the voting section of the school. Heaven only knows what he had been doing. He insisted on thanking every one of us standing at the door, then went happily on his way.

An irate lady came out of the voting room and marched straight up to me at the door. 'They won't let me vote! Wot can I do abaht it?' she demanded.

'Well, are you sure that you are on the voters' list?' I asked, already looking for a way out.

'Of course I am! I filled in the form mumfs ago!'

'Yes, but are you sure that you have come to the correct polling station?' This usually works: ninety per cent of the people who complain they have not been allowed to vote have turned up at the wrong polling station.

'This is *my* polling station. Look, 'ere's me card!' With that she produced her polling card.

' 'E said I couldn't vote. 'E said it was illegal and I'd git meself arrested. 'Ow can that be?'

There was nothing for it, I would have to go back with her to the presiding officer. 'This lady claims that she has been told that she can't vote. She says that she lives here and that this is where she always votes. Is there some problem?' I asked wearily.

'The lady *has* voted,' said the presiding officer, simply.

'Have you?' I asked her, sharply.

'Well, *I* 'ave, yer!'

'Well, what's all this nonsense about not being allowed to vote, then?'

'It's not fer me, it's fer me old man. 'E's at 'ome painting the kitchen. If 'e leaves it ter vote, I'll never git 'im back ag'in. 'E more 'an likely'll go round ter the pub. If 'e does that I'll never git me bleedin' kitchen painted. So I said to 'im that I'd come dahn an' vote fer 'im.'

'But you are not allowed to do that,' I pointed out.

'Why not? We're British citizens, ain't we? 'E fought in the last war, my old man did, yer know.'

'Yes, I somehow thought that he might have done,' I answered, almost to myself. In a much louder voice I continued. 'Look, you cannot vote on your husband's behalf, or anyone else's for that matter. People have been sent to prison for that!'

43

'It's an offence against the Representation of the People Act,' said the presiding officer. 'It's really quite serious.'

The lady now looked totally bewildered. All that she had actually wanted was her kitchen painted. Now she had visions of being thrown into jail. 'Ow, awlright, then, I'll tell 'im 'e'll 'ave ter come dahn 'imself. But 'e won't like it, 'e won't 'arf lead orf, my Ron will.' She shook her head in puzzlement and walked out of the door muttering to herself, 'I'll never git the bleedin' fing painted nah.'

'Would you care for a cup of tea?' asked the relieved young man.

It seemed like a very good idea.

Shortly after the departure of our attempted double-voter, I decided to return to the station for my meal-break. This had not been my original intention; I had in fact brought some sandwiches to eat on the premises. Voting, however, had been so light that the day had become quite boring. Just for a change of scene, I decided to return to Wharf Road to eat.

As I left the voting room, I could hear raised voices coming from the entrance lobby. My first impression was that Ron's wife had returned. However, on closer approach, a debate appeared to be taking place between the Labour poll-card collector and the Social Democratic courier.

'There's the copper!' exclaimed the Labour man. 'He'll know, let's ask him.'

'There's no need to ask him. I tell you, I am right,' responded the Social Democrat confidently.

'He reckons', said the Labour man, 'that I am not allowed to wear the name of my candidate on my lapel badge. Is that right?'

'Of course it is right!' snorted the Social Democrat. 'It's an infringement of the Representation of the People Act. The Act clearly defines that while rosettes *may* be worn, names are definitely taboo within the precincts of a polling station. Isn't that so?' He addressed the last words to me.

First, I did not have a clue, and secondly, I was getting just a little fed up with having the Representation of the People Act being continually thrown at me. I studied both participants for a moment and decided that the Social Democrat looked the more sure of his facts.

'Oh yes, that's quite correct. Names are definitely out – within the precincts of any polling station that is. The Act clearly states it. I'm a little surprised you didn't know that,' I added, somewhat daringly. I now looked at the courier in a new light. My first impression of him had been that he was a right wally, but now it was just possible that he might have outbluffed the pair of us.

I went for tea having heard enough about the Representation of the People Act to last me a lifetime.

It was while I was in the middle of a bad hand of brag that I was approached by Peter Cage.

'When your polling station closes at ten o'clock, no nipping round to the Sutherland for a quick pint. You are to escort your presiding officer and the votes to the counting centre at Peckham Girls' School. You can also pick up the presiding officer and the votes from Newington Church Hall on the way. I bet that makes you feel really important, doesn't it?'

'No, it bloody doesn't! What time am I going to get off duty, then? I'll be stuck down that school for half the night! I have a wife and child to go home to, sergeant. I crave my family's company.'

'Your "child" is now twenty-one! The only female company that you'll miss at ten o'clock is the barmaid from the Sutherland. If you hold them cards a bit differently you can get a flush on the last hand!'

45

'How am I going to get back?' I persisted, as I rearranged my nine cards.

'There'll be masses of transport there! You'll go in your presiding officer's car and pick up the Newington officer and her votes in the same car. Once at the centre, all you have to do is to hand them over to the senior police officer present and that's you finished. It's as easy as that.'

I returned to my polling station deep in thought. I had had a few sad previous experiences of escorting votes to the counting centre. The return of a weary constable in time to sample a pint before the pubs shut is very low on the list of the average police commander's priorities. My meditations were interrupted by a loud commotion coming from the direction of St Mark's School. Oh no! I thought, don't tell me that I am about to experience more aggravation with the sodding Representation of the People Act! As I came closer, I could see that it was nothing like as complicated as that. It was just Timothy McShutey – and he was very drunk. He was not only drunk but he was covered in posters! He had them on his head in the shape of a hat, on his chest and pinned on his back.

'Vote Harman, sur, vote Harman!' he called out as soon as he saw me.

'What's all this "Vote Harman"? You wanted Margaret Thatcher to win this afternoon!'

'Oi've changed since then, sur!'

'You've changed, all right – you're pissed! You can't run around a polling station like that! Take them posters off!'

'I karn't, sur!'

'Why not?'

'A fellah gave me a fiver in the pub, sur, to wear them, sur!'

'Well, whatever else he was, I bet he wasn't a Labour

46

supporter. I should think you've almost cost Harriet Harman the election! Now listen, take off them posters and go home. Do you understand me? You are very drunk and you're creating a disturbance, so hop it!'

'Why don't you nick the silly old prat?' came a hard voice from the other side of the road.

I looked up quickly to see Tim's son Benny striding purposefully along the opposite pavement. He was on his way to Wharf Road Police Station, where he 'signed-on' daily as a condition of his bail. 'Hey, Benny,' I called. 'Take your father home, otherwise he's certain to be in trouble!'

'Serves the old ponce right. If he's got drunk it's his fault. Nick him, he's asking for it. He's nothing to do with me!'

Benny indifferently carried on with his journey towards the station but his attitude incensed his father. In a fit of frenzy he began to tear the posters from his clothing and he hurled the pieces at me! 'You want the posters, sur? You can have the fooking posters, sur!'

'Here we go again,' I thought, as I called on my bat-phone for the station van. Although the van took only a few minutes to arrive, Tim had quietened appreciably by that time.

'I'm sorry, sur, I'm really sorry, honest I am, sur.'

'If I take you home, Tim, will you promise to stay indoors?' I asked him.

'I whill, sur, I whill dat, sur.'

'All right, but if you set just one foot outside, I'll cut it off! Understand?'

'Not a foot, sur, not a foot I won't, I swear by the Holy Mother I won't, sur.'

I helped Tim into the back of the vehicle and sat alongside him. The van then sped us quickly to his address some three streets away. Tim spent the short time apologizing for his behaviour. Never once, though, did he mention his son. We soon arrived outside 99 Chapter Street and I took the key from his pocket and led him up the nine steep steps to his front door. I eventually mastered the knack of turning his key and thrust him into the passageway.

'Right, here's your key and I don't want to see you for a week, understand?'

'Yes, sur, right, sur, you won't see me for a week, sur,' he agreed.

I slammed shut the door and ran down the steps. I got into the police van via the still-open rear doors.

'He's already come out again,' chuckled the van driver.

'What! I'll kill him!' I put my head out and, sure enough, there was Timothy standing at the top of the steps. He looked for all the world as if he was preparing to jump.

'Will you go in!'

'Yes, sur, yes, sur. I just thought, sur, that I'd like to buy you two fellahs a drink. It won't take a minute, sur!'

Drunk though Timothy was, the expression on my face must have penetrated his stupor. Before I had reached the first step, he was inside the house and had slammed the door shut tight.

'Where to now?' asked the van driver.

'Back to the polling station before that idiot comes out again.'

We roared out of Chapter Street and within a couple of minutes I was safely back inside St Mark's.

'I understand you are escorting the votes to the count centre,' said the presiding officer on my reappearance.

I nodded.

'Well, what's going to happen about an escort for Newington's votes?'

'I'm escorting you both. She's coming with us, isn't she?'

'No, she wants to take her own car. She says that she

doesn't want to come all the way back here once the count is over. You can't blame her, that's quite understandable, isn't it?'

Understandable it might have been, practical it wasn't! Each presiding officer was responsible for his or her own voting boxes. In turn, I was responsible for the two presiding officers. How could I then escort two people in two separate cars, neither of which I was driving?

Suddenly I saw an answer to all my problems. My own car was parked barely a hundred yards away. If I used it, I could escort them both to the count centre *and* arrive back before the Sutherland shut! All I had to do was to drive behind one of them and in front of the other.

At five minutes to ten, after a boring and inactive evening, the staff began to close up shop. The poll-card collectors had long gone, every newspaper had been read, and, for the first time for fifteen hours, the kettle was cold. The polling-station signs were taken down and the cubicles folded.

Suddenly, running footsteps caused everyone to look up. Dashing into the lobby was a tall West Indian youth.

'I'm not too late, am I?' he panted.

Each of our watches displayed a different time. However, the school clock was adjudged to be referee and it still showed fifteen seconds to ten.

'If we didn't close till three in the morning, there would always be someone who'd arrive with seconds to spare,' said the presiding officer, ruefully.

The last vote was then dropped into the box and the wax seal was set in place. Five minutes later, I ran for my car as the presiding officer sat warming up his engine.

Newington Hall was less than half a mile away. A tweed-suited, pearl-necklaced, round-faced lady stood tapping a heavy foot at the doorway. She looked like the madam of a

Cotswold Hunt brothel.

'Are you coming with me?' she offered, invitingly.

'No, luv, I have the other presiding officer parkèd just up the road there.' I pointed at a revving Austin-mini. 'I will follow him and keep you in my rear-view mirror. Okay?'

'Well, all right, I suppose.' She paused thoughtfully for a moment. The mini's revs grew louder. 'It's just that my battery is not too great. You may have to give me a push. That's actually why I asked if you were accompanying me,' she confessed.

I placed the voting box into the rear seat of her Ford and, true to her fears, her car battery was quite dead.

'If you wouldn't mind?' she pleaded, looking coyly up from her driving seat.

I gave my being-late-for-the-Sutherland sigh and heaved against the rear of the vehicle. We slowly gathered momentum and, after a few jerks and jumps, a spluttering of blue smoke gave way to a deep roar. Her silencer was not a lot either! Two more great revs and she was away. So, unfortunately, was the mini. In fact the only immobile object was me − and I was supposed to be between the pair of them! I do not know whether presiding officers are specially trained at Le Mans or are given private access to aviation fuel, but I never saw either car again.

Fifteen minutes later, I scoured the large car park at the count centre. There was no trace of either vehicle. Both should have arrived by that time. I reversed out and raced back to Newington Hall, panically studying every approaching vehicle. The hall was in total darkness without a sign of life anywhere. Once again I turned and frantically drove the two desperate miles to the centre. By now the car park was full and I was forced to park in a side street. I raced across the main Peckham Road, still putting on my helmet and buttoning my tunic. Traffic swerved around me and passers-by stared in amazement. I ran up and down the line of parked cars. Not a sign of either vehicle.

Perhaps both drivers had been hi-jacked by some terrorist group? But then that was nonsense, who would want to hi-jack 3000 votes from a safe Labour constituency? How about that SDP man? Yes, it could be him, I thought. Him and his bloody Representation of the People Act. I bet he feels he has lost the election and he's legged it with half the votes! What the hell would I say to the commander? 'Sorry, sir, but I've lost three thousand votes!' They would have to hold another bloody election. I could just see the newspapers, they would have a field day! 'Met Police Rig Election'! I wondered if I would have to pay for it.

The consequences were too embarrassing to contemplate, they just had to be here somewhere. I entered the counting hall and amidst all of its customary noise and confusion I spotted the commander instantly. I was about to approach him – any delay would, I supposed, be considered unforgivable – when I saw a tweed suit similar to that worn by my Cotswold madam. It disappeared again into the crowd. I weaved my way through the mass of officials in the centre of the hall and yes, there they were! The pair of them were standing calmly chatting to one another.

'Where the hell did you two get to?'

'We might ask you the same question. You were supposed to escort us,' she reproved.

'Escort you! I couldn't bloody well catch you!'

'Er, yes. I'm sorry about that but I was worried that my car might stall again.'

'But where are your cars?'

'Oh, we took a short cut and arrived at the back gate. Unfortunately it was closed for security reasons, so we left our cars there and walked round to the front. Would you care for a toffee?' she asked, offering me the remains of the day's sweets.

I declined the offer and, almost sick with relief, walked away.

'Are all of your votes safely in?' asked the commander, as I walked by in a trance.

'Er, oh yes, sir. Yes, quite safely in.'

'No problems?'

'No problems, sir, no. No problems at all.'

I looked up at the school clock – quarter past eleven. What had Peter Cage said, 'No nipping round to the Sutherland for a pint'? Well, he had been right about that. Oh, I hate licensing laws!

## Balzups

Rachel Wiezenberger had taken the tray of rings from the shop safe and was in the process of returning them to the window display. Sometimes she wondered why she bothered to open the shop on Thursdays. The fifteen-mile drive from Edgware to the Old Kent Road in rush-hour traffic was daunting enough, and then to open the place for just four hours seemed quite ridiculous. Simon, her late husband, had always insisted it was bad policy for a shop to be closed while the rest of the street remained open. But Rachel was tired. Early-closing day was a four-hour chore that she could well do without. She had carried the shop practically single-handed for the last five years. Rennie, a local mum, came in during school hours, but there was no doubt at all that the long-established family business was slowly winding down.

The old brass bell above the shop door clanged and Rachel waited expectantly for Rennie's cheery 'G'day, Mrs Wheezy'. She knew that Rennie would then spend the next ten minutes eagerly reciting the latest exploits of her daughter Tracy. She was a good worker was Rennie, but she most certainly could talk.

When after a few seconds there was no 'G'day', Rachel instantly perked up. Must be a customer — and at nine-thirty in the morning! Perhaps this was going to be the start of a very good Thursday.

Rachel carefully lifted her head from the display and

backed stiffly away from the window. 'I must get something done about this hip,' she thought.

A young, slightly built West Indian had entered the shop and was closing the door carefully behind him. He carried a small sports holdall which he quickly unzipped.

'Yes, sir, what can I show you?' She smiled a greeting. The smile became a contortion as she found herself looking down the double barrels of a sawn-off shotgun.


'That's the fourth armed hold-up on a south-east London jeweller's in the last six weeks,' pointed out Detective Sergeant Reg Kean that afternoon in the crime-squad office. 'All of them have been committed on a Thursday and each robbery has been carried out by the same man, in exactly the same manner.'

'Why on a Thursday, I wonder?' asked a colleague thoughtfully. 'Do you think that he might work in a shop himself that is closed on Thursdays? Many shops are, you know.'

'Well, at least we now know what he looks like,' answered Reg. This last reference was to the fact that although Rachel's jewellery shop was old and antiquated, it did possess one remarkable piece of modern equipment – a video recorder. There in front of them on a small video screen was the Thursday threat to south-east London jewellers'. But who was he? No one had yet recognized him so he was probably free of previous convictions. Well, he would turn up sooner or later, thought Reg, they always did.

Some weeks had passed and so had four more robberies, when a very promising young trainee detective walked confidently into the CID office. He took an equally confident seat at Reg Kean's desk.

'I hear from my informant that Collins the jeweller's in

Campton Street is going to be hit next Thursday morning!'

'Who by?' demanded Reg. 'Not our Thursday villain, surely? There are quite a few people work in Collins. I think that would be a bit ambitious even for him.'

'Well, yes and no. He'll be there all right but so will two of his friends and they'll each be carrying shooters. That's the information that I have received and it's always been good in the past.'

Kean had to agree there. He did not particularly care for the young man facing him, but in his comparatively short time at the station this recruit had built himself something of a reputation as a first-class thief-catcher, and had amassed himself a collection of very reliable informants. He had also just passed his selection board and was awaiting his official transfer to the CID. That lad was going to be a flyer, if ever Kean had seen one.

'Well, if it's going to be a heavy team, I suppose that we had better get prepared. You're absolutely positive about this, I suppose? There's absolutely no chance that your man could have made a mistake?'

'My man? No, not at all, sarge. My man is the business!'

'Hmmmmn!' Kean thought for a while. 'Look, I'm sorry, but I must speak with your informant myself, there's too much at stake for me to take an unnecessary chance. D'you mind?'

'Not at all, sarge.'

A few minutes' discussion with the informant soon convinced the detective sergeant of the quality of the information. Yes, this could well be the best chance they would get. Kean decided that the best way to approach the situation would be to hit the jeweller's the following Thursday morning, with just about as much force as he could muster. He further realized that the present strength of the CID office would not be enough if guns were to be used: he needed at least three, preferably four, authorized police-marksmen. He would obviously have to consult with his detective chief inspector but there was no doubt that if he wanted outside support, he would have to indulge in a little horse-trading.

Thursday the ninth dawned bright and clear. Fifteen men attended a secret briefing in the detective chief inspector's office. The uniform branch, always the last to be told anything, had sensed that something big was in the air, but as yet they had no idea what it was.

At 9.20 am the entire team left the station: fifteen men, four cars, six guns and a motor-cycle. Detective Davey Martin, who enjoyed a sense of the theatrical, had actually squeezed his slightly built frame into a size fourteen misty-blue frock! It was in fact Davey, swishing past the front of the jeweller's, who first spotted the small notice in the window: 'Closed all day Thursdays'.

Television programmes do at least prepare a recruit for the disasters that await him. Within an hour on the small screen, a crime is committed, investigated and solved. It is practically always neatly packaged. The hunter and the hunted are invariably known to each other and everything is smoothly arranged. It is very much like a black and white jigsaw puzzle. All the viewer has to do is wait until the very last piece drops tidily into place.

Reality, of course, is totally different. First-class Sherlock-Holmes-style detectives are as rare as hedgehogs at an orgy. Possibly fifty per cent of police investigations are disasters to one degree or another. This rule does not apply solely to crime; it applies to every aspect of policing. It will hit a recruit like a bucket of swill, almost as soon as he leaves the training school.

For my first few weeks as a recruit, I suffered the attentions of one Jock Bremner from a neighbouring beat. This spotty-faced nonentity latched on to me for about a month. He was a totally humourless character and found the police force very hard going indeed. For anyone without humour, life in the force can be very unkind. Time after time, a copper will feel that if he does not laugh, he will either resign or run home screaming. Jock Bremner did both. I sometimes feel quite guilty about my contribution to this.

Jock was very fond of recruits, solely because he found it easier to assert his small-minded authority over them than over more experienced people. He would switch his shallow allegiance as each new recruit arrived at the station. The fact that few men with more than six months' service ever spoke to him was an indication of his popularity. Jock attached himself to me one cold spring evening as I patrolled along Red Lion Row. This row was a narrow, gloomy road which ran parallel to the main road shops and served the rear of most of them. Between the main road and Red Lion Row was a derelict old cinema which was due for demolition within the next few weeks. During the day the place was a playground for kids, while at night it was a haven for drunks and last-line prostitutes. With piles of rubbish everywhere and gaping great holes in the floor, it was a potential death-trap. This particular evening was especially dark, and the rain that had been falling for some hours had streamed its way through the dozens of holes in the huge roof. Jock's intention was to enter the building through a broken door, then to roll and smoke a cigarette in the comparative dry of the auditorium. I decided that this would be a perfect opportunity for me to part company with him and carry on patrolling my beat, rain or no rain.

'Look!' he exclaimed dramatically. 'A fire!' He

pointed through a gap in the rear door of the cinema.

I bent forward and could indeed see a small bonfire at the far end of the building, with shadowy figures silhouetted all around it. 'It's only kids,' I said. 'They've got a small bonfire there. We'll make them kick it out.'

'Kick it out! Look, laddie, I'll creep inside and drive them oot and ye'll stay here at the door and capture them!'

'Capture them? But it's only a little fire. Why can't we just kick their arses out of it?'

'This could be arson,' he said, severely. 'Ye canna let arsonists get awhay wi' it!'

'Well, it don't look like arson to me – but go on, then, I'll wait here.'

Jock squeezed between the gap in the door and he was soon lost to my sight as he disappeared into the pitch-black of the cinema. All was silent for a couple of minutes, then I suddenly saw a flurry of movement among the silhouettes at the bonfire. Four young boys aged about nine or ten came rushing out of the gap. With some difficulty I managed to lay hold of two of them.

'We ain't dun nuffink, mister, 'onest,' came the six words that I would hear about four times a week for the next thirty years.

I held my two urchins for some ten minutes while waiting for Jock's return. Their protestations became more and more vociferous until we soon reached the pinnacle of protest of any Walworth kid: 'On me muvver's life, we ain't dun nuffink, mister.' Pretty strong stuff, I was thinking, when I was surprised to see the somewhat apprehensive return of the two lads who had originally escaped me. They did not come too close but stood a respectful six yards away.

' 'Ere, mister,' said the braver of the two. 'There's a man in there.' He pointed to the door. 'An' 'e's fallen dahn an 'ole. 'E's yellin' 'is bleedin' 'ead orf!'

'What do you mean, "He's fallen down a hole"? How do you know that?'

'Tha's why we run away, mister. We wuz jes' standin' rahnd the fire doin' nuffink, weh dis geezer yells at us an' falls dahn a bleedin' great 'ole! 'Onest!'

I was suddenly very alarmed. I bent forward and put my head into the gap and listened intently. Yes, there it was, there was absolutely no mistaking that guttural Glaswegian accent.

'Right, stay here, you lot!' I commanded as I dramatically burst through the door.

I ran for all of four yards then skidded panic-stricken to a halt. If Jock had indeed gone down a hole, then at the rate I was going I would very soon be joining him. I crouched down on all fours and peered slowly all around me. The bloody place was full of holes! They were everywhere − it was like being in a minefield! The kids, of course, knew them all intimately. Jock obviously didn't.

'Help! Help! Somebody help me!'

I skirted around two small holes before I came to a gap some five feet across. It was bisected by a nail-ridden, four-inch flooring joist. Hanging from the joist was a helmetless Jock Bremner and he was not very happy. The first problem was how to get him out. It was like a hole in the ice: I was not sure how safe the edges were. I decided to stick to the section of the edge that covered the joist, which seemed much more secure than anywhere else.

'If ye can put yer tunic over yon nails, I can make my way hand-over-hand along the joist,' he panted.

I quickly removed my tunic and spread it out as far as I could over the sharp protrusions. Jock swung his legs to gather momentum, and at that precise moment my tunic slipped from the joist. The emission of numerous Scottish oaths did not distract me as I peered anxiously down the pit.

'Hang on for just one more minute!' I encouraged, as I turned and carefully picked my way towards the bonfire. I picked a glowing piece of timber from the embers and returned to the swinging Scot. I blew fiercely on the wood, covering Jock with sparks, but two small flames flickered quickly into life. I could clearly see a bundle of clothing lying almost at his feet, while a few feet away a police helmet lay impotently on its side.

'Jock, you're only about six inches from the basement floor. Just let go and drop down!'

'But how'll I get up again?'

'There *must* be a way up.' I looked quickly around and blew once again on my wood. 'How about that staircase for starters?'

He groaned with pain as he released his hold from the joist. I picked my way to the staircase to meet him. Blowing continually on the wood, I felt I had every excuse for not responding to his bad-mannered questioning.

We emerged into the comparative brightness of the gloomy street. With our raised voices and Jock's bleeding hands, we must have looked like a pair of brawling drunks.

'And what ha' ye done wi' yon kids?'

'The kids? Well, I told them to wait.'

'Ye surely didna expect them to?'

'Well I never thought about it. But I could hardly have marched them in, could I? All they have done is what any sensible kids would have done – they've buggered off! If you hadn't rushed around pretending that you had some crown-case of arson, you wouldn't be in the state that you're in now!'

I thought he was going to hit me, but he didn't, and within a few weeks he had resigned. His shift breathed a sigh of relief and thanked me profusely. I thought that Jock

Bremner's falling down a hole would be classified as a rare occurrence, but in the everyday annals of police disasters it rates scarcely a mention.

It is a common practice for television writers, in particular, to portray us street constables as complete buffoons; whereas the so-called professionals – CID, vice squad, drug squad, Sweeney etc. – will be shown as super-efficient. Yet it is precisely these groups that have the greater potential for balzups. Take Peter, for example.

He has spent a sizeable chunk of his twenty-five years' service on such matters as unlicensed gaming clubs, brothel-keeping and drinking dens. He has worked much of the West End and a large part of south-east London. With his experience, nothing should go wrong; he should have every eventuality covered. In fact he thought that he had when, together with Sergeant Matthews, he staked out an allegedly small brothel in a Camberwell block of flats.

The layout of these flats made observation extremely difficult. The confidence of the caretaker was therefore sought and he provided the pair with keys of a nearby empty flat. Both officers then kept the suspect door under observation for almost two days, seeing no one go either in or out. Not wishing to waste any more time, the duo decided to take a chance. Tiptoeing up to the door, Peter knelt down on the mat and ever-so-carefully lifted the flap of the letter-box. Almost as slowly, the door began to open and, even more slowly, Peter fell forward into the brothel. There are, of course, numerous ways to enter such an establishment: authoritatively, seductively, even sensitively, but probably the least impressive of all is headfirst on your knees. Peter, however, was nothing if not professional. He had spent a fair period of time researching on the flat, just in case of an emergency. He now had such an emergency. Looking up at the brothel-owner, who was standing with the door knob in his hand and a puzzled expression on his face, Peter then produced his getting-off-the-hook card.

'I'm from the council, mate. I've come about the water leak that you reported.'

'The water leak?' echoed the astonished brothel-owner. 'Bloody hell, that was fixed two weeks ago, we've got fleas now!'

On returning to the station, the pair immediately deleted that particular establishment from the pending file. After all, as the embarrassed Peter quite reasonably explained, any brothel that is short on water and strong on fleas is hardly likely to be the scene of too much debauchery.

It is no doubt the heat and confusion of the moment that is primarily responsible for most of these disasters. After all, the only information that the fast-approaching police car may have about a delicate situation is the address '1 Acacia Avenue' – and the single word 'disturbance'. The average police emergency message is notoriously short on detail. A cool, clear head and an ability to step back and take stock would prevent most of these calamities. Unfortunately, the tendency of most coppers is to dive in and grab the first thing that moves. This approach is arguably responsible for some of the best, certainly the bravest, police work. It also makes for some magnificent balzups.

Not long after I had reached the exalted rank of area car driver, my radio operator accepted a call to a robbery on Clapham Common. The common was at that time the haven of many prostitutes, or 'toms' as they were more usually known by police. These women were all at the end of their service and nightly walked the badly lit common, simply because they dared not be seen in the daylight. It is a fact that any area that harbours prostitutes will also harbour the voyeurs, sad creatures whose only thrill is to watch others. In point of fact they usually see very little, although they will imagine a great deal. In addition to these peepers there were occasionally also ponces, gentlemen who lived off the girls' earnings in return for offering them some degree of protection. In the main, however, Clapham Common toms earned barely enough money to keep themselves. If any of them did possess a ponce, then he was invariably as far over the hill as they were. Last and by no means least – because there would, after all, have been no business without them – were the punters, or clients. Most of the business was arranged on the common during the hours of darkness. This well suited the anonymity sought by these men, who could only work up sufficient courage after the pubs had closed.

Threading their way through this tangle of ponces, prostitutes, peepers and punters was the occasional innocent member of the public. This could be someone who had innocently taken a short cut across the common, or was looking for somewhere to spend a penny after the public toilets had shut. Whatever the reason, among all the shady characters who lurked and paraded, there would be just the occasional good guy.

The sex act itself might take place in the back of a car, but more often on the grass – a location that might have been all very well on dry summer nights, but during damp foggy autumns and freezing cold winters it could have been no fun at all. The only option left open to the participants, therefore, would be against the slope of some suitably angled tree. This position was not without a great advantage: one elderly south London lady magistrate always maintained that sex between two standing people was impossible. Therefore, the offence of

63

'outraging public decency', which usually applied in open-air sex cases, was invalid when that particular magistrate sat in court. All sorts of reasons circulated as to just *why* this particular lady considered standing sex to be impossible. I have heard policemen claim that when she had once attempted it in her youth she fell from the two bricks upon which she had elevated herself. It was of course impossible to discover the truth of this theory, except to say that she certainly did suffer from puffy ankles.

The robbery call to the local area car had been brief: 'Clapham Common, north side, suspect chased by police'. The common is some distance from the Wharf Road manor but we happened to be in the area as a result of enquiries from a previous call. Within a couple of minutes we had reached the common but little was visible from the main road. I stopped the car and wound down my window. In the middle-distance it was just possible to discern two running figures before they completely vanished into the dark.

I drove the car up on to the pavement and decided to chance a journey across the common itself. 'Chance' it was, because the surface was pitted with holes and bumps and covered with mud from recent heavy rains. As soon as the wheels touched the grass I knew that I had problems. The vehicle began positively to waltz its way across the common. I switched on the full-beam headlights and instantly picked out the two running figures. The nearest runner was a tubby, helmetless figure who appeared to be in the process of giving up the chase. The other seemed equally tubby but infinitely fitter, and he was beginning to open up an appreciable gap.

'There they are!' exclaimed Bootsie Hill, my radio operator.

'Hang on, Boots,' I said. 'I'll get as close as possible and swing across the front of him!'

64

The runner then changed direction, veering sharply away to the left. I momentarily lost him as I frantically swung the steering wheel, only to find the car continuing to slither straight ahead. Suddenly the rear end of the car swung away to the off-side and I was instantly back on course. He was now tiring rapidly and as I drew alongside him, Bootsie began to open his door. At that moment, an unseen hole caused the car to swerve slightly, and through Bootsie's open door I heard a sickening thud followed by a pathetic moan. Bloody hell, I thought, I've killed him!

We leapt out almost before the car had stopped and Bootsie and I rushed to the fallen figure. Another groan from the body at least informed me that my worst fears had not been quite realized. If that sound had made me feel any better, this relief was instantly dispelled by the fat running copper.

'You fucking great idiots,' panted Tubby. 'He's the fucking victim! He was *chasing* the suspect!'

Bootsie and I stared at each other in a fair degree of panic. We looked down at the prostrate figure, then away into the enveloping darkness that now sheltered the long-gone robber.

'Do we move him?' asked Bootsie.

'Well, you can't leave the poor sod there, he'll suffocate in the mud!' snapped our fat friend.

Gingerly I bent alongside him. He suddenly lifted his head and spat out a quantity of mud and grass. 'I, I think I'm okay, thanks,' he panted.

'Are you quite sure? You had quite a fall,' I enquired, anxiously. Perhaps I would not appear in the dock at the Old Bailey after all!

'Yeh, yeh, I'm all right. Something thumped me in the back of the legs and threw me over. I'm okay, really.' He quickly felt both legs. 'At least I think I am.'

We pulled him to his feet and made pathetic attempts to brush him down. All we really succeeded in doing was to spread the mud around a little thinner. I went to the boot of the car and removed some pieces of old rag that were used to wipe over the bodywork from time to time.

'About the best I can do,' I apologized. 'Look, we'll take you into Clapham Police Station. We'll report the crime and you can clean up a little. How's that?'

'Yeh, thank you very much. That's very kind of you.'

Very kind? Well, yes, I suppose that if it is very kind to smash a victim of a robbery into the ground then suffocate him with mud and grass, we had indeed been particularly generous. However I could not help wondering what we had to do to be mean.

I opened the back door of the car and assisted the unfortunate man into a seat. The still panting constable had retraced his steps in an effort to find his helmet. Bootsie resumed his position at the R/T set and I slid into the driving seat and switched on the engine. Bootsie was now chatting pleasantly to our passenger who was now beginning to smile just a little at his misfortune. I selected second gear in which to pull away, believing it would be more effective on the loose surface. All that happened was that the engine roared and the car slid slowly sideways. I stopped the vehicle and tried again. This time with even less success.

'I'm sorry, but we're stuck. I'm afraid you'll both have to get out and give me a push-start.'

I received the expected oafish reply from Bootsie but our victim seemed quite philosophical about the whole thing. We were then joined by our fat policeman and the three of them took up a position at the rear of the big Wolseley.

'Once we get going, I'll not dare stop again. I'll wait for you all at the roadway, okay?' Only the victim acknowledged and that was with but the slightest of nods. 'If you push very hard, I'll try third gear this time. Right, here we go! Push hard . . . NOW!'

There was a slither, a splutter and a scream, and the car zig-zagged its way towards the distant roadway. I bumped down the kerbstone and waited patiently for the trio to join me. I felt they took a surprisingly long time to reach me. Bootsie was the first to arrive.

'Have you got any more of that rag in the car?' he asked casually.

'No, why? D'you want to wipe your feet?'

'No. I just thought that you may need to wipe them.' He gestured to the two approaching figures. Each sported a new tract of mud. It ran the entire length of their bodies. The victim had by this time barely a square inch of his face left unsplattered.

'What the hell happened?' I yelled at Bootsie.

'You're what happened! You and your crack-brained idea about push-starting the bloody car! They stood on each corner and I was in the centre. As soon as the wheels began to fly around, they disappeared under about four ton of Clapham Common. You wait till you see the state of them! I think that fat copper is gonna kill you!'

I clambered quickly out of the car and met both parties just as they reached the edge of the common. I can honestly say that I have never seen anyone in such a state as that victim. The clinging wet mud that festooned his person reflected the light from the yellow street lamps. The stout policeman was helmetless once again. He looked at me in such a manner that I thought nervously of Bootsie's prediction. He certainly looked angry enough to kill. I began to shape an apology, but he cut me short.

'Don't you say a word to me, d'you understand? Not one

fucking word! Get the both of us back into Clapham nick so as we can clean up as soon as possible.' He paused to spit a small stone at me. 'This poor sod's not only had his wallet nicked but you've bloody nigh killed him – *twice*!'

I opened my mouth to say that perhaps they should remove the worst of the mud before they climbed into the car, but then I thought better of it.

Some forty minutes later, after the robbery had been entered in the crime book and the night-duty CID had managed a quick interview, I waited in the R/T car to take home our treble victim. His face and hands were now almost clean but his blue-striped suit appeared to be made of compost.

'Where d'you live, guv?' I asked, helpfully.

He gave me an address in Brixton just a few minutes' drive away. I spent those few minutes apologizing. Eventually I stopped the car outside a small row of terraced houses.

'Look, don't worry about it,' he said, as he prepared to leave the car. 'You didn't do it on purpose and there's nothing that can be done about it now. I don't want any more fuss made and I would like to forget the whole thing. It's just that with the greatest will in the world, I don't think that I'll ever bother to send for the police again!'

We watched the victim climb the six steps to his front door, where he turned and gave us a forgiving wave.

'That comes of taking calls on someone else's ground,' said Bootsie. 'It could never have happened on the Wharf Road manor.'

'Why couldn't it?'

'We haven't got a bloody park!'

Sometimes in the making of a good balzup the potential disaster is soon spotted by other officers. These men, for a variety of different reasons, don't simply allow it to continue, they actually help it to gather momentum. One such victim of this attitude was Sergeant Timothy McHuffley. McHuffley must have had *something* that those who served with him failed to see. Before he retired from the force he had reached the rank of superintendent, which would have astonished anyone who had ever worked with him for longer than one week. McHuffley had three main faults. One, he was obsessed by never making a mistake. Two, he never considered that he had actually made one. And three, he never listened to anybody of a lesser rank than himself. (On reflection, perhaps this was after all a pretty good philosophy for a fairly rapid promotion.)

It had been a particularly busy night at Wharf Road. There had been the usual queue of customers at the enquiry counter and around twenty prisoners had been brought in by the night duty. Every corner of the interview-room, charge-room, surgeon's room and waiting-room contained at least one constable scribbling frantically away.

As the hour neared 6 am, it was fairly obvious that not every charge could be completed by change-over time. On occasions such as these, the early turn station officer will assist by clearing up the outstanding charges. It was now some thirty minutes after six and McHuffley was still busy on the station typewriter. 'Go home, sergeant,' said the early turn inspector. 'All of the prisoners have now been charged and there's only the bail to be attended to. The early turn station officer will do that little task for you.'

Through the open charge-room door, McHuffley could see a tall moustachioed prisoner waiting at the charge-room desk. This man had been discovered some hours earlier attempting to break into a local off-licence. All the necessary bail checks had been carried out on him and he was now only waiting for his property to be restored to him before he was released. McHuffley himself had charged the man. He doubtless thought that if he now returned the property, it would neatly round off the whole job. McHuffley had many quirks, none greater than that pertaining to prisoners' property. He did everything three times. He checked, double-checked and then, frequently, would do it all over again.

Also during that evening, a tall Syrian had been arrested for drunk and indecent. This man could speak little or no English. For some reason, McHuffley thought that Maxie Frazer, a well-known Walworth shop-breaker, was Eli Ben Wasif, a Mesopotamian drunk. PC Ronnie Fisher picked up the fifteen pound notes from the charge-room desk. He pointed out to Maxie that just as soon as he signed for his fifteen quid, he could go home. 'Just a minute, Fisher,' came the sound of McHuffley's weak voice from the front office. 'I'll do that for you if you *don't* mind. If anything goes wrong with property it always bounces back on the station officer. We must make sure that this prisoner fully understands exactly what is happening.'

Ron was about to say that Maxie knew as much about signing for property as anyone in the station. On the other hand, he had previous experience of McHuffley and he knew that the sergeant would take very little notice of him. He shrugged and watched McHuffley with only marginal interest. As the sergeant walked into the charge-room, he reached out and took the fifteen notes from the PC's hand. He then turned his attention to the prisoner and stared him straight in the eyes.

'Right ... pay ... attention ... now,' he said, very slowly and deliberately. 'I'm ... going ... to ... count ... this ... money ... understand?' Maxie nodded in genuine puzzlement. 'Right ... here ... we ... go. ...'

He picked up the first of the pound notes and waving it in a grand arc, ceremoniously placed it on the table in front of Frazer. 'One ... yes ...?' He then picked up the second of the notes. 'Two ... okay ...?' One by one he carefully went through the whole of the bundle. Maxie's eyes were opened wide as they followed each movement with incredulity. When the sergeant had reached the last note, he again spoke to the prisoner.

'Right ... now ... wait ... a ... minute. I'll ... do ... it ... again.'

Quickly picking up the notes he began to repeat the whole ritual: 'One ... two ... three....'

The arcs became increasingly large and even more deliberate. As the last of the notes rested on the table-top, McHuffley swept them quickly up and crammed each of them into Maxie's back trouser pocket. 'That's ... it ... now ... they ... are ... all ... in ... your ... pocket. Happy ... now ... ?'

Maxie turned and looked at Ronnie Fisher for guidance. Ron was having none of it; he raised his eyes away from Maxie to the ceiling and thoughtfully scratched the back of his neck.

'Now ... you ... do ... understand ... all ... that ... don't ... you?'

The prisoner turned to McHuffley and said in a worried tone, 'Yer, I've got it all right, sarge. But what the fuck is it, black magic?'

McHuffley wheeled around to the constable. 'I thought that this man came from Syria, Fisher?'

'No, sarge,' responded the po-faced Fisher. 'The Old Kent Road.'

The more dramatic the setting, the greater seems the balzup.

We had suffered a particularly horrific murder on the Wharf Road manor. A young Greek priest had been kicked to death while protecting his church from thieves. (Strictly speaking, that is not quite true. Being kicked to death while protecting your church from thieves is *not* murder, according to the courts: it was apparently manslaughter.) Information had been received that a suspect for this sickening crime lived in a small block of flats, just off the Wharf Road manor. However it could not be ascertained exactly which flat the suspect lived in. Almost every occupant of these flats had form (previous convictions), and the only way to obtain any useful information was to stake out the entire premises. To complicate matters, these were not particularly easy flats to stake out. There were no convenient vantage points where an officer could gain access. It was therefore decided to use a rather nondescript van for the observations. This was fitted with a two-way radio and left parked near the address, with two CID officers secreted uncomfortably in the rear. A small hole was cut in the floor for toilet purposes but apart from that little amenity, there were no other creature comforts to be had. One of the great enemies on any observation is the weather. In the height of summer one cooks; in the winter, of course, one freezes. This particular observation followed true to that tradition. It was a bitterly cold spring, so the two Wharf Road detectives wrapped up as best they could and settled down for a long wait.

After a few hours, the cold had permeated every joint in their bodies. In addition to this discomfort they had another problem – their cover had been blown! Someone in the flats had smelt a rat and a dozen or so people had emerged. They were now furiously rocking the vehicle. This was an excellent moment to call for help. However, any policeman who has ever performed operational work in an observation van will know that he can rely on one thing. At moments of great need, the radio will *never* work. This was indeed a moment of great need. In fact, when the leader of the mob was heard to say, 'Let's set fire to it,' the pair inside the van would have been hard pushed to think of a greater one. After several spluttering attempts at transmission, the detectives gave up and decided to sit tight and brave it out. They could not even drive the van away because the driver had taken the keys. It was now a question of time. Would some form of unexpected help arrive before the van went up in flames?

'If they do manage to set fire to us,' said the white-faced Detective Winters, 'I just hope that I don't have to go to hospital.'

'Why on earth not?' asked his companion, as he frantically scanned the street for help.

'I've got my wife's tights on,' came back the shy reply.

The 7th Cavalry never made a more welcome entrance than that of the Wharf Road van investigating the prolonged radio silence. Mrs Winters's tights, had however, already secured their rightful place in the annals of the Great Walworth Road Balzups.

## . . . and Wind-ups

Chief Superintendent Winchester took two seconds out from his paperwork to glance anxiously up at his wall-clock. Half past two! He had an appointment at Scotland Yard at three-thirty, so would need to leave the station at three o'clock at the very latest if he was to arrive on time. A chief superintendent could be as late as he liked at his own station where he was king of all he surveyed, but at Scotland Yard his rank was ten-a-penny. Even a chief superintendent has to be on time for a deputy assistant commissioner's conference.

A familiar rap on his door told him that Ted Donaldson, his uniformed administration sergeant, required a word. Ted was all right up to a point but he did have an uncomfortable knack of deputing work. Winchester had always been under the impression that police stations should be run by their chief superintendents and not their clerks. Donaldson, however, had the administration job so well under control that he could deal anyone at the station a paperwork body-blow at a moment's notice.

When Winchester had first joined the force, there had been one civilian clerk at his old nick and paperwork had been bearable. Now he was in charge of his own station, he had forty-three civilians, five uniform clerks and it was bloody nigh impossible.

'Come in, Ted, but don't bother me. I've got to be at Scotland Yard in an hour and I've got papers up to my eyebrows.'

'Yes, sir. I just wondered if you could squeeze in a quick AQR for a young recruit.'

'No, I bloody can't. I've got more than enough to do as it is. Superintendent Dawson is back from leave on Friday, let him do it!'

'The lad's going away for three weeks, sir, and his AQR is already a month overdue. You must remember the commander's memo about late AQRs, sir? You were going to do it last week but you put it back. By the time the lad comes back from leave it will be almost two months late. It won't take long, sir, it's very straightforward. He's a very straightforward young man.'

Winchester sighed in frustration. The AQRs, or Annual Qualification Reports, are a foolscap-size pen-picture of every officer in the force. The senior rank at each station must complete one annual report on each of his men, usually on the anniversary of their joining the force. These reports are a source of great amusement among the lower ranks, but they doubtless keep someone in employment at Scotland Yard. The idea of such reports is great in theory but less so in practice. On my twenty-ninth year of service, for example, the chief superintendent was supposed to discover if I was happy in the force and where I saw my career leading me. My request for a transfer to the underwater search unit was totally ignored. A friend of mine actually received his AQR after he had handed in his resignation on completion of thirty years' service!

'D'you think I can knock this report off in –' Winchester looked quickly at the clock and did a rapid calculation, 'fifteen minutes, say?'

'Of course, sir, easy. You'll be able to do this one in far less, I should think. He is *very* uncomplicated, this boy.'

'Well, that's a bloody change, I must say,' muttered the

chief. 'Every bloke that I've had up here recently has either got some poor cow up the stick or wants a transfer to MI5. All right, show him in. Oh, by the way, what's his name?'

'Dobbin, sir, PC Dobbin.'

Winchester grunted, 'Some of the bloody names we get in the job nowadays! Once it used to be Taff Evanses and Arthur Browns. Now it's Juliens, Darens and bloody Dobbins!'

'No, Dobbin is his surname, sir.'

'I know it is, you fool! Look, don't waste my time. I'm down to twelve minutes now. Show the lad in and let me have his file.'

Donaldson pulled the door to and the chief superintendent waited impatiently for the recruit to make his entrance. He cast his mind back to when he, too, was a young recruit waiting to see his guv'nor. 'I bet his old tummy is churning over,' thought Winchester, nostalgically. He then slipped into the part that all chief superintendents love to play. He lowered his head to his paperwork and ignored the entrant for a few moments. He then frowned importantly and slowly looked up in a preoccupied manner. He had used the ploy so often that his timing was absolutely perfect.

He had heard the door open and been aware of the heavy footsteps on his new gold carpet. Must be a big lad, this one, with footsteps like that. About time we had a few big coppers in the force. Some of the recruits that we get nowadays look like midgets with clubbed feet. He then heard the door close tight behind Constable Dobbin. Funny, I can't place him, though, thought Winchester, as he raised his head in the traditionally approved, chief superintendent head-raising manner. He then all but had a coronary. There, standing quite still in the middle of his lovely new gold carpet, was a real live donkey, with a plastic policeman's helmet nestling neatly between his ears!

He rubbed his eyes in disbelief. It was still there! It was a donkey right enough, but what the hell was a donkey doing in the chief superintendent's office on the second floor of a building that did not possess a lift? I hope he's bloody tame, thought Winchester, as he slowly moved around the room towards the door. The donkey, although standing quite still, followed the chief superintendent with his great sorrowful eyes.

'Whoa, boy, there's a good boy, whoa.' He reached out and nervously patted the animal's head.

He finally reached the door and opened it slowly, continuing to look apprehensively over his shoulder at the animal. Putting his head out in the corridor, he could see Sergeant Donaldson and several CID officers rolling about in the main office.

'Donaldson! If you don't get that brute out of my office in two minutes flat, you are on night duty tomorrow night – and for the next ten years! Get rid of it now, d'you hear?'

The giggling group tried desperately hard to control themselves as they squeezed past the chief superintendent and entered his office. Not only did it already smell a little like a stable, but PC Dobbin was concentrating very hard on urinating on the new gold carpet.

'How did you get that bloody animal up here in the first place, sergeant?'

'With great difficulty, sir. It took five of us to persuade him up the stairs!'

'Well, you will just have to persuade the stinking brute down again. You can also pay to have that new carpet cleaned. Good God, man, is that the time? I've got to be with the DAC in thirty minutes!'

77

'Tell him that you had to give a donkey an AQR, sir. I'll bet that'll impress him no end.'

'I'll be back about six-thirty and I do not want to see one trace of that animal, do you understand? Not a trace!'

'Sir!'

As Chief Superintendent Winchester slumped wearily into the back seat of the station's general-purpose car, he could think about little else except Donaldson's wind-up. I bet he's hugging himself with pleasure, he thought. While Winchester enjoyed a joke, even against himself, he was a little angry for leaving himself so wide open.

As it happened, Ted Donaldson was anything but pleased. If he and his CID accomplices had experienced difficulty persuading the creature up the stairs, it was nothing compared to the problem of how to get it down.

'Look, this is a race against time!' said the sergeant to the rest of his gang. 'If he has pissed on the carpet, you know what is next, don't you?'

The plain-clothes officers did not need a second telling. They decided the only way to return the creature to ground level was to blindfold him and carry him down the staircase manually. For that they needed plenty more help. But while camaraderie among the force is usually second to none, the general reaction to this particular request was 'You took him up, you take him down!'

Eventually, one or two men weakened sufficiently to come to the sergeant's aid, and a little after four o'clock the animal was at last led quietly across the station yard. Donaldson's genuine dread of the donkey fouling the staircase proved groundless – Dobbin did it in the corridor.

Just before 7 pm the chief superintendent returned. The donkey appeared to be none the worse for wear as he munched cheerfully away in the corner of the station yard.

There was not, of course, a supply of donkeys kept at the station solely for winding-up guv'nors. It was simply that Dobbin's owner, a local totter, was currently incarcerated for thieving lead.

While it is unusual for a chief superintendent to be the victim of a wind-up, no one in the force is considered to be totally immune. Recruits, of course, are absolutely made for it.

My own introduction to these leg-pulls took place during my first period of night duty. It was there that one young man happened to mention he possessed a couple of budgerigars, named Sidney and Rita. Nightly he extolled the winning ways of these cute little pets. Soon everyone on the shift became sick to the teeth with the daily adventures of Sid and Reet. Eventually two old coppers took him confidentially to one side and asked him if he had ever given a thought to the manufacture of marcasite jewellery. It could, they pointed out, be a very rewarding hobby. The young man agreed that doubtless it could be, but how on earth does one make it?

'By baking budgerigar shit at a pretty ferocious temperature – that's how,' they whispered.

Well, mused the young man, I have the ingredients, all that I lack is the means. Given sufficient thought, he did not feel that this could be too much of an obstacle.

Mr Hall, the popular Walworth baker, was quite astonished by the strange request that he received from the fresh-faced constable. 'Who in their right mind,' he said, 'wishes to place great dollops of budgie shit in the same oven as my long crusties? I'd get closed down!'

'It makes wonderful marcasite jewellery,' persisted the young man.

'It makes bloody awful bread,' responded the baker. In spite of the young man's entreaties, Mr Hall was adamant.

There were to be no budgie deposits in his ovens.

Another great idea, it seems, bit the dust for the want of a little initiative.

Many years later, the same young man had risen high in the ranks of the force. He became, in fact, the personal body-guard to Princess Margaret. I often wonder if, on those long car journeys, he regaled Her Royal Highness with nostalgic stories of Sidney, Rita and marcasite brooches.

At Wharf Road in recent years 'B' shift (or 'reliefs', as the shifts are more commonly known) specialized in the really big wind-up. Every recruit will, sooner or later, undergo some bizarre task. This assignment will doubtless cause him to wince each time he looks back on it. 'B' relief does not, of course, have the monopoly on wind-ups. These leg-pulls are practically a force tradition. It was just that theirs were usually so inventive. All over the Metropolitan Police area, it is a fair bet that some poor soul will be struggling through a daft scheme devised by a couple of bloody-minded older plotters. Take the customary force 'whistle test', for example.

A recruit will be sent out, usually in the early hours of the morning, to the most barren part of the manor. There he will be instructed to stand still on some small hill or mound. At a prearranged time, he will then be required to give numerous long blasts on his whistle. This is, so he is led to believe, to assist the special MI5 listening devices to be re-tuned. Or perhaps it could be a scientific test of the whistle volume itself. This would, of course, be made purely for con-stabulary research purposes. Whatever the reason given, you can be fairly sure that on every day of the year, somewhere in London, a rosy-cheeked young recruit will be standing on some hump, blowing his lungs out. Heaven only knows how many wide-eyed nightwatchmen have been frightened out of their wits by the sight of such a copper in full blast.

Diverting though these capers may be, they pale beside the force-famous 'B' relief pigeon-shoot. This 'shoot' carved out a place for itself in the annals of Wharf Road wind-ups.

Running parallel to the Walworth Road and alongside our police station is the elevated section of the Blackfriars to south London railway. The scores of rusty old railway bridges which bisect this line are a haven for hundreds of grimy-grey London pigeons. Judging by the deposits on the pavement, these creatures exist solely on a diet of Guinness and prunes. Periodically they reach pest proportions and the local council then employ a controller to shoot them, usually with a rather powerful air-rifle. Now anyone wandering the streets banging away with rifles in the early hours of the morning must, of necessity, be of some constabulary interest. The council therefore notifies each police station a day or so before a shoot is due to take place.

'B' relief were late-turn that Thursday and Walter McClean was still exploring the wonders of being a south London copper. Walter had come up from deepest Dorset and was finding the layer of London that lies just beneath the visible surface rather difficult to fathom. His first problem had been the language. He never seemed to know what anyone was talking about. He could not understand them and they could not understand him. As far as Walter was concerned, all cockneys should have sub-titles. Traffic, crime – the whole pace of life seemed to be different from anything that Walter had ever experienced before. His problem was not, of course, unique – most country kids need a period to adjust – it was simply that Walter was needing longer than most.

The relief was lined up just prior to commencing their tour

of duty and Sergeant O'Toole was reading out the local informations.

'Council notify us that the customary pigeon-shoot will be taking place on our manor within the next few days. . . . One of our local villains is over the side from Ford open prison. . . .' O'Toole droned on as he waded through the routine notices.

'A pigeon-shoot!' thought Walter. Now that really was something that he knew about. He quite missed the old countryside sweeps into the guns each autumn. Of course pigeons do not have the glamour – or the taste – of pheasants and partridges, but even the thought made him feel quite homesick.

As the relief filed out into the chill Walworth air, Walter made his first big mistake. He turned to Alan Sinclair and said, 'I didn't know you had pigeon-shoots in London, Alan. How on earth is it done?'

Now Alan had some fiendish streak in his make-up that enabled him instantly to spot the possibility of a good wind-up. He could not at this early stage work out exactly what form the wind-up would take but he sensed that the ingredients were there. All he needed was time.

'Well, if you're really interested, I'll see what I can do for you,' responded Alan. 'Of course, you don't have very much service in the force – but leave it to me, I'll work something out for you.'

'Thanks, Alan, thanks a lot,' said Walter, gratefully.

By the time the shift had paraded for Sunday's late-turn duty, the great 'B' relief pigeon-shoot had been worked out to the very last detail.

The biggest threat to the wind-up would lie in the number of commitments that the station was required to fulfil. Fortunately, there were few marches through central London that day. The manpower at Wharf Road was therefore left fairly intact. This was imperative, because several men would be needed for the task.

As Sergeant O'Toole read out the Sunday afternoon postings, he stopped when he came to Walter's number. 'Ah! 927, I've got a special job for you. Stay behind after parade and I'll tell you exactly what it is you are to do.'

'Sergeant,' acknowledged Walter proudly.

Later, in the parade-room, O'Toole explained just what Walter's task was to be. 'About 5 pm, just after it gets dark, you are to go to the top of Vestry Road. There you are to face north and walk slowly down the centre of the roadway. On your right-hand side, you will see Lucas Gardens. Now vast numbers of pigeons have taken to roosting in the trees in these gardens and it will be your job to flush them out. You will use your personal radio because we have wired up the gardens with stereo equipment. You will need to walk slowly, and every two or three yards I want you to shout "Bang-bang-bang" into your transmitter.'

'Well, how about the traffic, sarge?'

'Don't you worry about it. We're going to divert it for you. On the north side of Peckham Road will be the guns. If the shoot is successful, then perhaps you will be allowed to take part in the actual shooting on the next occasion, although usually we like a man to have at least five years' service before we allow him to use a gun in a public place. Right, off you go. Give us a call on your radio when you reach there, all right?'

'Yes, fine, sarge, thanks!'

During the twenty-five minutes that it took Walter to reach the top of Vestry Road, half a dozen men were scattered around the surrounding streets to divert the traffic. This did not make a great deal of difference to the flow because there were numerous alternative routes. It was, however, thought to be imprudent to allow cars to race down the hill if a young constable was wandering along the centre of the carriageway making pronounced 'banging' noises. The problem for the jokers would arise at the bottom of the hill: there, Vestry Road ran at right-angles into Peckham Road which was always an extremely busy thoroughfare.

Eventually, with everyone in position, Walter called up to indicate that he was ready to wake the sleeping pigeons and drive them into the guns.

'Okay,' called back O'Toole, 'let it rip! The louder the better!'

Slowly Walter made his way down the hill, but, sadly, to no avail. Not a feather stirred among those slumbering pests. He was met at the bottom by O'Toole who was sitting patiently in the police van, together with Alan Sinclair.

'Sorry about that, Walter,' said Alan, 'but the GPO are having all sorts of trouble with the sound. You'll have to do it again. Go back up the hill and this time bang this bin loudly.' With that, he handed over to Walter a large, grey, metal bin. A length of well-worn sash-cord made a makeshift handle. 'You'll find it a lot easier if you hang it around your neck. You needn't shout this time – just bang the drum.'

Walter looked dubiously at O'Toole.

'Yes, it's quite okay, Walter,' reassured the sergeant. 'I do realize that it's a bit of make-do-and-mend but it's the best that we can do in the circumstances.'

Walter grinned a little sheepishly as he slung the cord around his neck and set foot once more up the hill.

'All right, are you in position, Walter?' called O'Toole on the radio. 'Right then, off you go – and don't forget, whack that bin as hard as ever you can!'

'He'll never do it!' said Taff Evans, the van driver.

'I bet he does,' responded Sinclair, confidently.

They all craned their necks as they listened intently for any approaching sound. All was quiet for the first couple of minutes, then each heard the sound of running feet. Emerging into the street lights just ahead of them was an elderly West Indian man. He rushed breathlessly and wild-eyed up to the van.

'Dere's an officer up dere an' Ah doan think he's very well. He's walkin' down de centre of de road bangin' a big rubbish-bin.'

'Oh that's all right, guv,' said Alan quickly. 'He's on a special exercise, that's why the traffic's diverted.'

The newcomer looked distinctly unimpressed as he stepped back against the wall and stared apprehensively up the road.

They did not have long to wait. Soon the deep booming of the front-office rubbish-bin could be heard as Walter bashed its base unmercifully. He looked expectantly at O'Toole as he neared the police van. The sergeant nodded and quickly gave him a thumbs-up sign as he eagerly signalled him on.

Alan had now stopped the Peckham Road traffic and the thumping Walter slowly emerged into the junction. The double stream of Sunday drivers could hardly believe their eyes as Walter crossed the wide road in full uniform still banging away on his 'drum'. Alan stood solemnly and expressionlessly in the centre of the junction with his arms calmly raised. He gave just a casual nod as Walter passed by and quietly whispered the word 'Good'.

The van now swung around and picked up Sinclair from the centre of the junction. O'Toole was in favour of extending the length of Walter's patrol the one and a half miles back to the station. Alan, however, knew that this would be pushing their luck. They soon caught up with the drummer and assured him of the success of the entire operation.

'That's funny,' said the puzzled lad. 'I didn't see one pigeon!'

'Didn't you?' exclaimed Alan. 'Bloody hell, there were hundreds of them!'

'Well, I never heard as much as one gun!'

'Well, you wouldn't, would you? They were using specially silenced airguns. Pretty powerful, I admit, but nevertheless – airguns!'

Everyone was soon picked up from their traffic points and later in the canteen the shoot was discussed in great detail.

It wasn't until the later part of the evening that Walter had occasion to walk past the huge trophy case that stood in the corner of the canteen. It contained a trophy that he had never noticed before. At first glance it looked particularly familiar. It was a grey metal bin with a sash-cord attached. There was a label stuck in the centre of the bin with an inscription thereon. It read: 'This trophy was awarded to Walter Pigeon for his part in the Great Wharf Road Pigeon-shoot of 1979.'

Sadly, Walter did not remain much longer in the force. I do not think the pigeon-shoot was the actual cause of his departure, but it certainly didn't encourage him to stay.

Many of these leg-pulls are impromptu, spur-of-the-moment jobs: an opportunity is discovered, then used to its best advantage.

Some years ago, our front-office enquiry counter at Wharf Road was a rather long affair that ran almost the whole width of the office. This old counter could be particularly chaotic at busy periods. There were frequently as many as a dozen people, all seeking some sort of advice. Privacy was therefore at a premium. Everyone was understandably pleased when the designers shortened the thing, from twenty feet in length to nearer five. Everyone, that is, except Sergeant Paddy O'Callaghan. It deprived him of his favourite party-trick. Paddy had a wind-up, usually played on a lone enquirer, that I never knew fail. The first time that I saw him perform it, I was as astonished as was the lady enquirer.

She had entered the front door and stood patiently at the end of the counter. She had apparently lost her dog and was extremely upset about it. Paddy removed the 'Dogs Found' book from the cupboard and laid it on the counter between the pair of them. He studied it intently while the lady also did her best to read it, albeit upside down. He suddenly looked up at her and their noses practically touched.

'Hmmmmm,' he murmured, almost to himself. 'I wonder if we have it downstairs in our dog-basement.' I was quite intrigued by this remark, if for no other reason that we do not possess a basement, dog or otherwise.

'Hang on a minute,' said Paddy. 'I'll go down and have a look.'

With that he turned and walked slowly along his side of the counter, bending his knees progressively more at each step. The result was that he became lower and lower as he moved along the counter. Yet it must have been quite obvious to the dog's owner that there could be no steps there at all. By the time he had reached the end of the counter, he was completely on his knees and totally out of sight. The lady hazarded a quick glance, by momentarily leaning forward.

'No,' said Paddy, sadly, 'it's not here.'

He then turned, not without difficulty, and began to 'climb' back up to the far end of the counter.

'Oh, thank you,' said the lady, backing away. 'Thank you very much.'

'Call back any time!' called Paddy cheerfully after her.

A few months after this basement walk Paddy was

transferred to Southwark Police Station, not, I hasten to add, for any sinister reason. It was there that he pulled the Great Royal Fishing Concession Wind-up. Yet again, it was a country recruit who found himself the victim.

Norfolk lad John Shinn had arrived at Southwark Police Station a very disappointed young man. London, to John, had always been St Paul's, Big Ben and the Tower of London. No part of John's mental picture of the great metropolis had ever featured the Old Kent Road, Bankside power station and the Tooley Street doss-house.

Unfortunately for John, he made his disappointment known to Paddy O'Callaghan. To compound this error, he further mentioned that his one great obsession in life was to fish. He was, in fact, a typical fishing bore.

'Did they not tell you about the Special Fishing Concession when you were at the training school?' enquired Paddy casually.

'No, no one mentioned it to me,' answered John, immediately showing great interest.

'Well,' went on Paddy, 'because some parts of London are far grottier than others, the Queen suggested that it may be a good idea to offer those men in the less fortunate areas certain concessions, one of these being a concessionary fishing right. Anyone who is a member of the Metropolitan Police in these particular areas is allowed by special royal decree to fish from selected royal ponds and lakes in central London during the hours of darkness. It has to be dark, you see, otherwise everyone'll want to join in.'

John nodded at that. After all, you couldn't have just *anybody* fishing in these royal waters.

'Now,' continued Paddy. 'Any copper who is posted to, say, Chelsea, Hampstead or posh areas like that is not eligible, but people like you are. That's fair, isn't it? Are you interested?'

'Interested! Arh, that I am, sergeant! I love a bit o' fishin', do I!'

'Good, well, all you do is make out a report requesting permission and give it to me. I'll put it through to the Royal Fishing Concession Office and within a week or so you should get your approval to go ahead. I suppose you do possess proper rods and things like that, do you? I mean, we can't have string, sticks and lumps of bread floating about all over the place, can we? The Queen don't care for that at all, and besides, it chokes the ducks!'

'Oh, no, sergeant,' responded the hurt John. 'My equipment is abser-lutely boo'tiful. You just tell me what I'm to put on my application, an' I'll do it right away.'

'Well, it's straightforward enough', said the sergeant. 'Address your request to Her Royal Highness The Queen, c/o Special Fishing Concession Office, Buckingham Palace. You'll have to put your measurements on the form − you know, height, weight and things like that. Some of the banks of these ponds can't take very much weight and you are quite a big boy. You'll also need to put in it the length of your rod and the weight of your lead. Oh yes, and any experience that you may have had. Let me have the application form just as soon as you can and I'll see what I can do for you.'

'Well, thank you very much, sarn't, that's very kind of you. I'm obliged.'

'Not at all.'

Two or three weeks later, O'Callaghan told John that his permission had finally come through. 'The only problem is that while you are doubtless a very experienced fisherman in Norfolk, you are an unknown quantity down here. You will have to do the statutory couple of hours in the "nursery pool", I'm afraid. I realize that it will be a bit of a come-down for you but you must appreciate the Concessionary Officer's position. They have to check absolutely everything before they dare let anyone loose on the really big fishing.'

'Arh, that's fair enough,' agreed John happily. 'What do I do now?'

'Well, on your very next night off you just report here, at this station, together with your rod, maggots and sandwiches. Fetch along every bit of your equipment so they can see just how well-equipped you are. It'll stand you in good stead when they finally decide exactly what lake you will be allocated to. One other problem is that there is nowhere to park near the Palace. If you just have a word with the station officer when you are ready to start, he'll arrange for the van driver to give you a lift up there. Okay?'

'Okay indeed, sarn't! Is next Tuesday all right? I'm orf duty then.'

'Next Tuesday'll be fine. Report here at midnight. I won't be here myself but the night-duty relief will be expecting you just the same.'

During the latter part of Tuesday evening, a steady rain began to fall across London. John Shinn thought he had better use his best waterproofs if he was to cut anything like a good image. Therefore, when he finally reported to the night-duty station officer he looked better suited to a four-hour combat with Moby Dick than a dabble in the waters of a London park lake.

Paddy O'Callaghan reluctantly decided that even the chance of witnessing the final stages of his wind-up did not merit a ten-mile drive into work. He therefore found two very able deputies in Sergeant Cummings and the van driver, Roger Kilroy. These two had decided that midnight was perhaps just a little early for the plot. The scheme, they felt, had a better chance of success an hour or so later. John spent this hour checking and re-checking his equipment. Finally, soon after one o'clock, the station officer spoke to the fisherman.

'Well, your approval has come through. You've been allocated to Victoria memorial pond for your nursery try-out. How do you feel about that?'

'I don't rightly know where that is, sarn't.'

'It's slap-bang in front of the Palace. If the Duke gets up for a "slash" in the night, you're going to be the first thing that he sees. So be on your best behaviour at all times, understand?'

'I certainly do, sarn't.'

'I doubt if you'll find much in the way of fish in that pond but then that's not the purpose of the exercise, is it? It is just to see how you handle yourself. You never know, if you are really impressive they may give you Regent's Park lake next. I hear that someone had a four-foot-long pike out of there!'

John positively drooled as he hurried towards the van.

Some fifteen minutes later, the vehicle rolled slowly to a halt at the memorial in front of the Palace. An 'A' division copper, on duty at the Palace and sheltering from the rain, paid only marginal interest in it: one police van is just like another. His interest, however, did increase when he saw a well-clad figure with rod, stool and umbrella alight from the rear of the vehicle. It increased even further when the figure subsequently sat on the stool and hung the rod over the bubbling fish-free waters.

The van swung smoothly away from the kerb and headed towards the main gates of the Palace. The lights flashed twice in quick succession. The Palace constable walked towards the railings as the van driver alighted.

'It's okay,' grinned the driver. 'He's fishing.'

'Not another one, surely?' groaned the foot constable through the railings.

'You mean you've had them before?'

'We get them all the time!'

'How long can you give him?'

'Well, no more than an hour. Have you given him a "permission form"?'

'Yes.'

'Okay, I'll go over a little later and tell him it's invalid. I assume that he has no transport back?'

'No, but he can walk it in three-quarters of an hour. It's all good experience you know. Cheerio!'

'Cheerio.'

They both looked across at the fisherman who was already engrossed in his cucumber sandwiches.

One of the risks run by any 'wind-up merchant' is the 'biter-bit' syndrome. Nothing gives greater solace to the smouldering victim than thoughts of suitable revenge. The big problem is that winder-uppers are devious by nature and therefore very difficult to nail down. A revenge was, however, finally wreaked on O'Callaghan.

One of the most difficult and arduous tasks within the force, is that of station officer at a busy station. The station officer is quite simply responsible for everything that takes place within the building. No matter what goes on, or frequently even doesn't go on, the station officer is held responsible for it. O'Callaghan took over as early turn station officer one spring Sunday morning. The night-duty shift had been particularly busy and there was still a great deal of work to be done. None of the overnight drunks had been bailed and once Paddy had settled in, this was to be his first task.

All the male cells were full but there had been no female

prisoners held overnight at all. Therefore one male drunk and disorderly had been housed in the first female cell. This was a fairly common practice, the only drawback being that if the list was not checked thoroughly the prisoner could be overlooked at wash-time or at breakfast.

Having worked their way through the male cells, O'Callaghan and the assistant station officer, PC John Ryan, decided to stop for tea and a slice of toast. By the time they resumed, it was about 7.15 am. The sergeant sat at the desk in the charge-room surrounded by papers while the PC disappeared into the corridor that housed the female cells. John Ryan was a quiet, undemonstrative type of individual. This was rather fortunate in the circumstances. He reappeared from the female cells after a few minutes looking extremely thoughtful.

'Sarge,' he said, scratching his head, 'I think we've got a bit of a problem with the last of the prisoners.'

Because John did not sound particularly dramatic, Paddy ignored him for a couple of minutes. He was, after all, very busy and he still had many entries to make in the charge-book. He finished the entry he was making and drew a neat red-ink line straight across the page. Putting down his ruler and pen, he then clasped his hands together and sat back in his chair.

'Now, John,' he said, graciously. 'What's the problem with him?'

'He's dead.'

'He's what!'

'He's dead. I think he's been murdered. Leastways, he's got a knife sticking out from between his shoulder blades.'

The chair crashed over as O'Callaghan leapt to his feet. He ran to the corridor and John Ryan walked thoughtfully along behind him. The small steel vent in the door had been slid completely open. The sergeant put his right eye to the gap and peeped into the cell. There, lying three-quarters obscured by the sleeping-bench, was a body. A stiletto-type knife protruded straight up from the shoulder blades. Blood was everywhere and the body lay ominously still.

'The keys. Quick, give me the keys!' John fumbled for a few seconds. 'Come on, man, the keys, give me the bloody keys!'

'They're not here, sarge, they don't seem to be on the ring.'

'What do you mean, "not here"? Of course they're bloody here! Give them to me!' In the passing of the keys, they fell to the floor. Paddy dived on them as he tried desperately to find the correct one. 'Quick, call the duty officer while I try to open this bloody door!'

'You'll never open it without a key, sarge, will you?'

'Well, give the night-duty station officer a ring at home. Find out what he's done with the sodding thing!'

'Oh, I don't think we can do that, sarge.' John looked at his watch. 'It's twenty past seven, he'll be asleep by now.'

'Asleep! Asleep! Do you think I sodding care if he's asleep? There's some poor bastard lying dead in there and we've got no keys!' Suddenly the full significance of the situation hit O'Callaghan. 'Do you realize that I've signed for him?' He pointed to the closed door. 'That bloody corpse in there is down to me. I've signed to say that he was in good health at six o'clock!'

'Well, judging by the state of him now, sarge, I should think he must have had rigor-mortis at five,' said John, unhelpfully.

Paddy yet again went through every key on the ring while John called up the early turn inspector on the bat-phone. 'Sergeant O'Callaghan has a problem, sir. He'd like you to return to the station as soon as possible.'

'Will do!' came the curt reply.

'Oy! What the bloody hell's going on out there? Can't you be a bit quiet?'

'Who said that?' exclaimed Paddy.

'It came from further down the corridor, sarge. It must have been in one of the other cells,' answered John.

Paddy ran down the corridor looking quickly into each empty cell. There, in the last one of all, was a sleepy drunk. He was sitting up on the bench and looking thoroughly cross.

'What're you doing here?' called O'Callaghan through the vent.

'What'm I doing here? Why, I was bloody nicked, that's what I'm doing here. This is just about the worst bloody police station that I've ever been in. There's been nothing but noise all night. It's more like a lunatic asylum. Can I have bail?'

'What's your name?' demanded the sergeant.

'Robinson, Arthur Henry Robinson,' said the bewildered man.

'Robinson!' echoed Paddy. 'Well, if you're Robinson, who's that in . . .' He paused and looked closely at John Ryan. 'Ryan! You bastard!'

John's inscrutable features did not at first alter. 'What's the matter, sarge?'

'Don't you "What's-the-matter-sarge" me! You know what's the matter all right!'

John Ryan's face finally cracked into a huge grin. 'Had you going, though, sarge, didn't we?'

'Where's the bloody keys?'

'The duty officer's got them.'

'Well, I'll tell you this,' said Paddy, with a sigh of relief. 'You certainly scared the shits outa me!'

95

The return of the duty officer with the keys enabled the cell door to be reopened. The tailor's dummy that had been found lying in the road after a break-in was removed. The tomato sauce and red ink was cleaned up and Arthur Henry Robinson was bailed.

'He who lives by the sword, sergeant, sometimes goes fishing,' said the smiling early turn inspector.

The wind-ups which give greatest satisfaction to members of the force are those that are really well planned and then perfectly executed. Inspector David Loosley was approaching the end of his two-year attachment to the pornography squad. (Twenty-four months is considered the maximum time that anyone can safely be exposed to such influences.) It had been Loosley's habit to inflict wind-ups on previously departing officers. It therefore followed that there would almost certainly be an attempt at revenge on Loosley himself. He was also fairly sure that he could avoid it. He would make a specific point of *not* reacting to anonymous phone calls. Nor would he 'report for a special task' while dressed as an Arab or a Turkish ponce: he certainly wasn't falling for that one. All he had to do was keep his head and he would emerge unscathed from his two years with the squad.

On his arrival at the office one morning he had discovered a rather official-looking letter from two specialists at a London teaching hospital. These celebrated gentlemen stated they were carrying out an experiment into the effects of long-term exposure to pornography. They requested the assistance of the Metropolitan Police in furnishing them with two suitable examples. One would need to be an officer who was new to the department, while the other should have a great deal of service. The inspector was not mentioned by name and the letter had been sent originally to the deputy assistant

96

commissioner's office. It had subsequently filtered its way down to the pornography squad.

At first, Loosley had some nagging doubts. He decided to check the letter for validity so telephoned the hospital and spoke to the research department. He was unable to speak directly to either doctor, but their secretary was extremely helpful and told him that the research team was eagerly looking forward to the experiment. The team hoped that both policemen could come along to the department as soon as possible. As a result of this conversation Loosley felt much more relaxed, and a few days later he and his colleague arrived at the hospital.

The young sergeant who had been at the squad for just a few weeks was tested first. Then it was Loosley's turn. The two doctors explained their theory to him then asked him numerous reaction questions. 'We will fire just one word at you and you answer with whatever comes into your head. It would be particularly helpful for our research if we could wire you up to this electrograph. We are very indebted to you, inspector, for your cooperation.' For the next few minutes, dozens of questions were fired at the victim with lightning speed. They were mostly to do with sex. The medical team then thanked him once more and he returned to Scotland Yard.

Some days later, a confidential report was leaked to Loosley. It stated that in the view of the research team, Inspector Loosley had been unduly influenced by his exposure to pornography. It further stated that any possible promotion should be postponed for some time, in order that he might adjust. Some quiet backwater of the force was suggested, where he could possibly recuperate.

These disclosures cast no small blight over his farewell office party, but after a couple of drinks he had recovered

some of his old bonhomie. During the course of these celebra-
tions, somebody claimed that they had in their possession an
extremely funny film. If it were projected on to the department's video screen, they said, everyone would be highly
entertained.

The guests all gathered around and made themselves as
comfortable as possible. Soon the small picture leapt
colourfully to life. There on the screen as clear as a bell was
Mr Loosley. But what on earth was he doing? He was wired
up in a chair, with a rubber cap on his head, answering quick-
fire questions about his sex-life!

It did not need the emergence of the two medical men for
him to realize the extent of the wind-up. It had involved the
whole of the pornography squad, half of the top brass at
Scotland Yard and the research team from one of London's
teaching hospitals!


It is not common knowledge that a rogue satellite once
landed on the grass in Peckham Rye. This information was
kept from the press for fear of alarming the public. One
problem for the police dealing with returning satellites is that
few forces have either the knowledge, or the means, to cope.
This, however, is not always the case. In the following top-
secret incident, I can now reveal that at least one man from
Peckham Police Station maintained the very highest stan-
dards of the force.

The first difficulty in dealing with any re-entering satellite is
recognizing it: few people really know what they look like. I
mean, unless you actually see one whizzing through space
and crashing into a fiery heap on Peckham Rye, how do you
really know it is a satellite? It could be anything. It could, for
example, be part of an old television set, wrapped in petrol-
soaked carbon paper and left lying on the Rye.

Perhaps if you were an enthusiastic young constable, you would need to have looked elsewhere for your confirmation. It is possible that you may have found it in the top-secret information that had been leaked to you, some four hours earlier. The station teleprinter had, after all, clattered out a pretty sinister message:

MAY ALL FORCES BE AWARE THAT THE UNITED STATES SATELLITE DANAE, IS IN IMMINENT DANGER OF BREAKING UP AND RE-ENTERING THE EARTH'S ATMOSPHERE. THE SATELLITE'S TRAJECTORY INDICATES THAT CERTAIN PARTS LARGE ENOUGH TO SURVIVE RE-ENTRY MAY STRIKE GROUND IN AREA ACROSS CENTRAL EUROPE, INCLUDING LONDON AND HOME COUNTIES. ALL SUCH UNTOWARD INCIDENTS ARE TO BE REPORTED TO OPS CENTRE JODRELL BANK OBSERVATORY IN ACCORDANCE WITH FORCE PROCEDURE. TOP SECRET.

This is pretty worrying stuff. Any constable finding himself walking near Peckham Rye in the early hours of the morning would obviously be well advised to keep his eyes wide open. As if this information was not distressing enough, an additional teleprinter broadcast was made an hour later at 2 am.

MAY ALL OFFICERS BE AWARE THAT INCIDENTS AT BOREHAM WOOD AND EDMONTON INDICATE THAT PARTS OF THE SATELLITE MENTIONED IN PREVIOUS MESSAGE HAVE STRUCK THE GROUND CAUSING DAMAGE. FIRST REPORTS INDICATE THAT THESE OBJECTS MAY BE RADIOACTIVE. SUITABLE EQUIP-MENT FOR HANDLING THESE ITEMS, NOW AVAILABLE AT ALL DIVISIONAL POLICE STATIONS. ALL ACTION TO BE TAKEN IN ACCORDANCE WITH STANDING INSTRUCTIONS. TOP SECRET.

Well, there it was. Science fiction had finally become fact –

and in Peckham! For the next three hours, our young constable determinedly ensured that the local population could sleep soundly in their beds. He maintained a determined, if fruitless, vigil. Suddenly, around five o'clock in the morning, the situation changed drastically. Again the teleprinter clattered.

EMERGENCY CALL PECKHAM RYE, NR KING'S ARMS PUBLIC HOUSE. EXPLOSION AND FIRE. MESSAGE TO MIKE FOUR.

This was followed a minute later by another burst on the printer.

EMERGENCY CALL NR KING'S ARMS PECKHAM RYE. FIERY OBJECT FALLEN FROM SKY. NO ANSWER FROM MIKE FOUR.

No answer from mike four! What could have happened to them? The sleek white Rover and its three male occupants were not responding to radio communication. Could the satellite – if that's what it was – obliterate all radio signals? Had something unspeakable happened to the crew? Perhaps the answer lay in the shrewd observation made by a more experienced constable: 'Clothing! Did they have any protective clothing?' Police cars carry a great deal of equipment, ranging from breathalyzer kits to the driver's sandwiches, but 'Divisional Satellite Collecting Equipment'? Sadly, no.

'I'll go up there and have a quick look!' said the brave young constable.

'Well, all right,' agreed his colleagues, reluctantly. 'But first we must prepare you.'

The Divisional Satellite Collecting Equipment was rushed to the brave young constable and he was soon dressed for his dramatic new role. Strangely enough, the DSCE radioactive-proof cape did bear a certain resemblance to the old-style uniform capes that went out of service some twenty years earlier. It was also true that the special DSCE rubber boots looked a little like the car-washer's wellies. As for the rubber gloves, well, that special DSCE anti-radioactive dust bore more than a passing resemblance to dried detergent. Finally, if one did not know better, one might have thought that the special DSCE anti-flash cap was a baker's hat.

With the complete DSCE now tried for size, all that remained was to transport the brave young constable to the scene. But how? With police radios rendered ineffective, how could a car be called for this purpose? Just a small snag this. With great dexterity, a terrified passing motorist was waved down and directed to the scene.

Sure enough, there on the grass, a short distance from the King's Arms public house, was the smouldering satellite. Any remaining doubts that the brave young constable may have had were quickly dispelled by the notice on the back of the satellite: SOLAR PANEL DIGITAL CONVERTER. Well, of course, that confirmed it. Anything that carries a Solar Panel Digital Converter just *has* to be a satellite.

It is surprisingly easy to extinguish smouldering space-satellites. They don't weigh much, either. In no time at all, the brave young constable, firmly clutching his satellite, was posing in the station for photographs. Not, you understand, for the press. After all, the whole matter was still a top secret. No, these photographs were simply for history.

Some day, perhaps, this story will finally be given security clearance. The brave young constable who saved the slumbering people of Peckham while dressed in car-cleaner's wellies and a baker's hat will be suitably recognized. Strangely enough, I hear that he wishes to remain anonymous. Ah well, of such stuff are heroes made.

# Thief!

In the summer of 1969, the Right Honourable Enoch Powell, MP made his dramatic Rivers of Blood speech, forecasting all manner of urban horrors. As a direct result of that prediction, the Home Office initiated the Community Development Project (CDP), which was to be set up in deprived inner-city areas. The idea was to stimulate local people into taking far more interest in their own welfare.

In Walworth, a team of six to eight workers, some of them part-time, were based in an old tumbledown semi-derelict shop. There they ran advice sessions, organized tenants' associations and helped with literacy schemes. They undertook just about any task that would make the lives of the socially deprived more bearable. They translated 'officialese' letters, queried gas and electricity bills and, in short, dealt with practically every form of domestic or civil rights problem. An organization like the CDP was not, of course, without its critics. The main opposition came, oddly enough, from an unexpected quarter – the old-style Labour councillors. There was no obvious reason for this, unless they saw it as a threat to their own standing in the area. While the project did have a number of faults, on balance I found them an enthusiastic group, which did genuinely good work with many people. For example, the project spent a great deal of time and effort with both young and old. They would take youngsters out in a mini-bus during the day, then in the evening the same bus would be used for the elderly. For me, the success of the project could be measured by the two weeks' holiday in Holland which one of the staff organized for seventy of our local kids. When I saw the names of some of those travelling, I remember marvelling that the Dutch dykes were still intact on their return, and that Holland was not at war with us within a week. Even more incredibly, many Dutch families who had accommodated the kids that year actually asked them back the following year! (Even some of their mothers wouldn't have done that.) It was on the basis of this last feat that I became a true project supporter!

This stance had its dangers for a community constable. If, for example, the project had become too strongly political, I could have been left in a very vulnerable position, looking at best naive and at worst incompetent. There was no doubt that a few of the project workers did hold strong political views. Yet by and large they went about their job of work and left their politics aside. This could not always be said for their opponents.

One wet evening, in a moment of weakness, I agreed to serve on a new committee formed by the project. A group of local people were trying to build an adventure-playground. There were two fairly considerable problems to be solved. The first was that there was no site, and the second — there was no cash! Some ten people, including a local councillor named Isles, who was elected chairman, formed the membership of the first committee. For me this looked a fairly innocuous task. I quite liked the idea of being involved in the community and I did not see how anyone could possibly object to my being on the committee. Our first meeting decided quite sensibly that before we did anything at all, we needed cash. Therefore, in an effort to raise some, a dance was arranged in the local church hall. This idea would have the extra advantage of giving some fairly cheap entertainment to the kids themselves.

The arrangements for the dance went off quite smoothly and everyone on the committee, with the exception of dear old Councillor Isles, busied themselves on the night. I decided that I would be best employed on the door. Nearly all of the kids attending the dance knew me and I thought that they might well find a policeman's presence inside the hall somewhat inhibiting. In addition, of course, life would definitely be quieter outside. I did, though, have a couple of slight reservations. These appeared when I saw two very well known faces queuing up for entry. The first was Danny Roberts, a sly, slim sixteen-year-old. In time of trouble, Danny was always there, or thereabouts. So far, Danny had always managed to evade the law, but his name was usually the last warning given by most mums to their departing offspring. '... and stay away from Danny Roberts, do you understand?' They understood right enough, but they still sought him out.

My second reservation was motivated by the potential bludgeon to Danny's rapier – one Michael O'Connor. Any attempt to describe the sturdily built, seventeen-year-old Micky would pale into insignificance beside the one I once heard from a veteran police dog-handler: 'Micky,' he snapped, in a fit of total exasperation, 'you'll never be anything but a real thick yob, never!' Well, Michael O'Connor had already fulfilled his early promise – he was now truly 'a real thick yob'.

The pairing of a sly plotter and an easily led nutter did not make for good chemistry at any teenage disco – and I stupidly let them in!

The next three-quarters of an hour lulled me into a false sense of security. Everything seemed to be going so well.

The interval had just taken place and tea, buns, pies and sandwiches were being sold by committee members upstairs in the canteen. Unfortunately, there were two accesses to the upper floor. Many of the kids began to bring their refreshments down to the dance hall. This was something that we had not foreseen. Although I did manage to stop any child coming down the exterior staircase, the interior steps were at the far end of the hall and our supervising staff were a little over-stretched. The paper plates were no problem but the china cups were a totally different matter.

As soon as the music began to play again, Mary Roach and Jennie Crane, two local mums who were on our committee, came out of the hall where they had been gathering up cups. 'There's something going on in there, Harry,' said Mary, with a worried frown. 'I don't quite know what it is but the girls are all at this end and the boys are all at the far end. There's definitely a bad atmosphere there.'

I peered through the door and could see instantly what she meant. At the opposite end of the hall I could clearly see Micky O'Connor and he appeared to be arguing with someone. For Micky to be arguing with anybody is a premonition of war.

I was just about to enter the hall, when I remembered my heavy leather coat. It had been quite a chilly day and because I knew that I would be spending some time in a draughty lobby, I had, possibly unwisely, brought along my most expensive garment. I had spent too many years policing the area to leave a highly prized coat lying around unguarded at a teenage dance. I quickly gathered it up from the back of the chair and dumped it into Mary's plump arms.

'Look after this for me please, luv. Take it upstairs and put it underneath the ... !' Screams and yells interrupted my sentence. I ran the five yards back to the door and the sight

105

that I was greeted with was amazing. Absolutely everyone at the far end of the hall seemed to be fighting everyone else. It must have been instantaneous combustion. I had been away from that door for all of twelve seconds and it already looked like the deciding battle of world war three! Cups, pies, sandwiches and chairs hurtled through the air. The rush of young girls out through the door threw me momentarily off-balance. The warlike scene was at direct odds with the Beatles record being played: 'Love, love me do!' I grabbed the first two kids to hand and they seemed greatly relieved for an excuse to stop fighting. I looked instinctively for Messrs Roberts and O'Connor. I did not really expect to see Danny but I was fairly sure I would see dear Michael. To my surprise, neither was in sight.

My attempt to restore order was greatly assisted by three or four of the mums who had raced down from upstairs as soon as they heard the commotion. They tore into the fighting boys and the battle was over almost as quickly as it had begun. There was food, broken china and glass everywhere. All the lights had now been switched on and there was barely a girl in the room. A sad little sight indeed.

I was absolutely furious, not least with myself. I should have been in the hall at the beginning. Or at least I should have entered without going back for my coat.

'C'mon, you lot!' I snarled. 'You can help clear up this bloody mess that you've caused.'

Jennie Crane's boy Darren had been in the thick of it. I was therefore quite pleased to see the powerful arms of Jennie dragging him out through the door with scant regard to his protests.

Slowly, and with the help of the new sorrowing participants, we tidied up the place. That was about the least we could do. Each of the adults felt a sense of guilt. We had taken up the offer of the church's hospitality and it had been abused. All of us felt that we could have done far more to have prevented this happening.

This did not appear to be one of my best nights. On the credit side – we had certainly raised a few bob. Just because everyone had left early was no reason to return any money. In addition, the fracas had not occurred until after the interval. Therefore, our sales from the refreshment bar had been quite good. However, on the debit side were the breakages – we would have to pay for these. There was also the blow to the committee's morale. The nagging doubt remained: if these were the kids for whom we were building an adventure-playground, then perhaps a long-stay prison would be a better bet?

The following Wednesday, the committee was scheduled to have another meeting. I was delayed in arriving that evening and when I eventually walked into the project's old shop, it was fairly obvious that something big was brewing.

'We've got the site!' blurted out Mary Roach excitedly, almost before I was in the door.

'Where?'

'On the corner of Bronte Lane and Gaza Court. It's the old slum-clearance site. We've been offered it for five years for just a peppercorn rent. Isn't that great! Oh! There's another bit of news too!' She left the sentence hanging ominously in the air.

'This second bit doesn't sound quite so good,' I said suspiciously. 'What is it?'

'Councillor Isles has resigned from the committee. He said, to use his own words, "It's over the disgraceful happenings of last Saturday night." But that's not of course true, is it?'

'Isn't it? Why isn't it? I wouldn't blame him if it was.'

107

'He's resigned because he lives in Bronte Lane, that's why! He lives about forty yards from our adventure-playground. Councillor Isles thinks it's a great idea to have an adventure-playground, unless, of course, it happens to be near him!'

'Surely not?'

'What other interpretation is there, then?'

Any doubts that we may have had concerning Mary's uncharitable assessment of Councillor Isles were soon to be dispelled. Within two weeks, he had not only resigned from our committee but had formed a committee of his own to oppose the siting of the playground in its allocated spot.

As the weeks wore on, groups of kids and voluntary helpers began to knock the playground into some sort of shape. Grants from charitable bodies were applied for and promised. Then, some four months later, the playground was officially opened.

If we had experienced complaints from Isles before the opening date, they were nothing to the dozens that streamed in once the playground was opened. This was slowly placing me in an impossible position. Isles would regularly complain to me about the nuisance that he claimed the playground caused. These complaints were always addressed to me as the local copper. He was therefore complaining to me in my official capacity about the direct fruits of my unofficial activities. The final straw came with the arrival of an anonymous letter addressed to the superintendent of Wharf Road Police Station. It complained bitterly about the playground and the hooligan elements who sheltered there, 'underneath the protective arm of the Metropolitan Police'. I now had no choice – I resigned and left the committee.

Several months passed and there were many other things happening on my patch, all of them needing attention. One of these matters concerned a smart old lady named Esther.

Esther Violet Wood had been recently widowed. She had also sustained two attempted break-ins to her one-bedroomed flat. This combination was well known to me and was not good: it was turning yet another elderly but able-bodied lady into a recluse. Esther and I became quite good friends and when she told me of her interest in local politics, I thought Councillor Isles could possibly help. There were two elections due within the next few weeks, national and local, and Esther thought that she might be able to assist. She added that she would like to collect the polling cards from the voters at the door of the nearby polling station. This task is not usually considered to be among the most interesting and volunteers are therefore extremely difficult to come by. The following day I spoke to Isles about her offer and he leapt at it.

I was very happy about this: I saw it as the first step to getting Esther mobile again. There was no doubt that Esther's mental state greatly improved after her two long and arduous sessions at the elections. She could now be regularly seen scurrying backwards and forwards to the shops, an exercise she had not undertaken for months. She also looked a great deal younger than her seventy-four years.

It was during one of my weekly calls on her that she first mentioned her son in Canada. She had nursed a twenty-year ambition to visit him before she died. She was obviously thinking that time was running out on her.

'Why can't you go, then?' I asked.

'I'm too old. And besides, I've never flown before.'

'Nonsense! People very much older than you travel for the first time. You're in good health and you can afford it. You'll never get a better opportunity.'

I sensed that she desperately wanted to be talked into the

trip, so I endeavoured to destroy her objections, one by one.

'I don't like leaving the flat for all that time.'

'How long *is* "all that time"?'

'Six weeks.'

'That's no problem. This flat is quite close to the station. I park my car practically outside your door. Why don't you go? I'll keep an eye on your flat while you're away – honest!'

She smiled. 'How would I get to the airport?'

'You can get a mini-cab all the way if you wish, or simply to the air terminal.'

'No, I don't think so. I wouldn't like those sort of people to know that the flat would be empty for all that time.'

I had to admit that she had a point there. It was amazing how many of our local sharks had gravitated to the mini-cabbing business. 'I'll tell you what, then. If that's all that is holding you up, I'll take you to the airport myself. How about it? You cannot possibly have any objections now, eh?'

'How about coming back?'

'Well, if you give me an exact time, I'll even meet you on your return. What d'you say? You'll never get a better offer!'

'All right. I'll write to my son. If it's okay with him, I'll fix a date.'

'Good! You just let me know when you need me to drive, and I'll be there.'

I called by again a week or two later and Esther excitedly gave me the date. It was to be the last week in October.

It was a bright autumn Thursday morning when I knocked on Esther's door. She had insisted that I parked my car in a neighbouring street. No one, she said, was allowed to know that she was going away. Her cases were fortunately not very heavy. At least, they weren't to start with, but by the time we had reached my car, they weighed a ton. I drove her to the west London air terminal and carried her cases into the check-in. I wished her a safe journey and checked her return flight.

'I'll see you in six weeks, Esther. Be good!'

'Just one minute before you go, will you take my spare keys and just pop in from time to time? I'd be so much happier if you would.'

I paused for a moment. Police discipline regulations expressly forbid the acceptance of keys covering one's place of duty. What the hell, I thought, the fact that I have driven her here puts her immediately into a different category to that covered in General Police Orders. She is more of a friend. Surely even policemen are allowed to accept a friend's key? I smiled at her and took the keys. 'Sure, Esther. Off you go now or you'll be late.'

I received a card during the third week of Esther's absence and she appeared to be enjoying herself immensely. My wife Joan, who had never actually met Esther but had heard a great deal about her, bought her a small Christmas present. It was just a small box of mixed groceries, to be left on her kitchen table as a surprise. Seven days before Esther's return home, I lay in Lewisham Hospital recovering from a heart attack. In those particular circumstances, some matters tend to get overlooked. I overlooked Esther.

It was towards the end of February before I returned to duty at Wharf Road Police Station. One of the first tasks to perform was to furnish Esther with her belated Christmas present. I felt quite silly carrying the Christmas-wrapped package, but on reflection I decided that the whole thing looked far more attractive with the paper than without. I had rehearsed my little speech and I walked up to Esther's door and gave an official-sounding rat-tat-tat. She always enjoyed that. I raised the package until it was almost at face level and prepared my little welcome-home-two-months-late address. I heard the bolt and safety-chain slide back and the door slowly opened.

I was aghast at the change in her. She had aged terribly. He face was drawn and hollow and her normally immaculate hair was unkempt and wispy. At first she did not seem to recognize me. Suddenly she recoiled: 'Oh! Oh! It's you!' She struggled and became panic-stricken in her attempts to close the door.

'Esther! Esther, luv, it's me. Harry Cole. You know me, PC Cole!' The door was now slammed shut and I heard the chain rattle into place. I bent to the letter-box and called: 'Esther! What's the matter, luv? Esther, are you all right?'

'Go away! He said I mustn't speak to you. Go away!'

I shrugged helplessly and walked thoughtfully back to the station. I was beginning to feel a complete idiot. It was 24 February and I was walking the streets in full uniform with a brightly wrapped Christmas present under my arm.

Next day, I called into the Community Development Project shop and cadged my usual cup of tea. As I sat chatting, I mentioned my encounter with Esther.

'Oh, don't worry about that,' said Margaret, one of the part-time workers, cheerfully. 'My children took her under their wing once and she turned on them in the same manner. She goes like that at times.'

I thought no more about the matter until the following Monday. I was about to leave for work when my telephone rang. It was a close friend of mine from Wharf Road Police Station.

'I've just heard on the jungle-drums, you've got heap big trouble.'

'Trouble? What sort of trouble?'

'From what I hear it's the worst. It's an allegation of theft.'

'Theft! That's ridiculous! Who? Where?'

'Dunno any more than that. It's all a bit hush-hush at the moment. All I can tell you is that an old lady came to the front counter with some councillor geezer. He said that he wanted to report a theft by a policeman. He was then shown straight into the inspector's office. Last I heard, he's in with the chief inspector. We didn't even know who it referred to until some time later. Apparently it's you.'

I sighed just about the biggest sigh I had ever made in my life. I didn't even realize just how big a sigh it was until some moments afterwards. By then I was too dejected to be impressed. The journey to work seemed to take twice as long as usual. A 2 pm start would normally ensure a traffic-free drive, but somehow today's trip took ages. I entered the front office and made to book on duty on the duty state. This is a detailed sheet that is kept in the front office of every police station and relates to everyone's duty times for each day. It is something like a factory time-clock, only in writing.

The duty state was not there. A bad sign this. It meant that the time and day referred to in the allegation was being checked against the time I was actually shown working. Every minute of duty time that I spent during the period covered by the allegation would be checked. If it failed to correspond with my officially listed time I was in trouble. I would be in trouble whether or not the allegation was substantiated. No policeman likes that sort of scrutiny, community coppers least of all.

I pointed out to the station officer that I could not book on because of the absent duty state. 'Guv'nor's taken it upstairs somewhere,' was his indifferent reaction. It was fairly obvious to me that he wasn't in on the act and on first impression it appeared that very few people were. Normally rumours fly around a police station at the speed of light. There is always someone at every nick who can spread scandal like wildfire.

113

If, however, a quicker circulation is required, then one simply tells the same story – but this time in confidence. The effect can be electric; no computer can match it. Well, there appeared to be no 'wildfire'. Perhaps it had all been a mistake?

There seemed to me little point in going straight out on to the streets. I would, after all, be summoned 'upstairs' fairly soon. I could therefore see no sense in dashing from the far corner of my beat for something that I was half expecting within the hour. I spent the whole day like that, and two-thirds of the next one.

Finally, at three o'clock the following afternoon, I received a call via my bat-phone. 'Return to Wharf Road and see the chief inspector as soon as possible.' I breathed a sigh of relief and immediately felt better. I now had a tangible enemy. Previously it had been an undercover campaign by an abstract opponent whom I was not even supposed to be aware of. Now it would be out in the open and I did not care who knew it. All I wanted to know was the exact allegation and who had made it. Nothing else bothered me.

The chief inspector was strictly polite and invited me to sit down. He told me that a Mrs E. V. Wood and a Councillor Arthur J. Isles had called on him and made an allegation of theft against me. Both parties had made written statements. The allegation was that during the six weeks that Mrs Wood had been away, I had entered the flat and therein stole a quantity of property. Namely, two plastic shoe-horns and four envelopes. He pointed out that because this was an allegation of theft by a serving police officer, the papers must therefore go to the Director of Public Prosecutions for his guidance. I was then invited to make a statement. I asked for two minutes to think it over.

The allegation against me was ludicrous. I knew it and

114

everyone who had anything to do with the case must have known it. I was fairly sure that included Councillor Isles. At first glance, my Achilles heel was the bloody keys. My being in possession of old Esther's keys was not a criminal offence but it was most certainly a strong discipline matter. Although no disciplinary action would be undertaken while criminal proceedings were being considered, it would come soon enough afterwards.

On balance, I decided to make a statement. While I would totally deny the theft, I would admit the entry to the flat with Esther's spare keys. My defence would be that I classified Esther as a friend and therefore our relationship was on a totally different footing to that covered in the discipline regulations.

'What was Isles's part in all this, sir?' I asked the chief inspector with genuine curiosity.

'He said that he felt that Mrs Wood needed moral support and as she had approached him in the first place, he simply decided to see the whole thing through with her.'

'What had she approached him about, for God's sake? That she couldn't get her shoes on and she'd lost her bloody envelopes? I bet he was over the moon! I can just imagine his delight. "So PC Cole has been in your flat, has he, Mrs Wood? And you've now discovered that your two shoe-horns are missing? It seems like he took shoe-horns from you and gave *me* a playground! We must do something about this, Mrs Wood, mustn't we?" For my money, guv'nor, Isles is a devious old bastard!'

'Would you care to put that in your written statement?' said the chief inspector icily as he brought me straight back to reality. I did not even bother to answer him.

I spent the next hour penning my statement. It was soon copied by the typist and I signed every sheet.

'What's my position now, guv? Am I suspended?'

'Not at this stage, although I suppose that could come later. At the moment, and until you hear differently, you can carry on with your normal duties. Just stay away from 148 Gripton Street. It is essential that you have absolutely nothing at all to do with this woman, understand?'

I nodded, although I resented being told anything quite as obvious as that. I muttered some thanks, although I was not at all sure why, and left his office. The most maddening aspect of the entire situation was that I knew I could resolve the whole thing in a five-minute chat with Esther. I also knew that it would be insane for me to attempt it.

I left the station at six o'clock that evening and walked into the neighbouring street for my car. I was so deep in thought that I totally failed to recognize the all-too-familiar figure that lurked on the pavement. Although I may have failed to recognize the figure, the voice cut instantly through my meditations.

'PC Cole, I'm sorry, really I am.'

'Esther!' I wheeled around on her. 'Esther! I cannot talk to you. Please go away!' I fumbled in two wrong pockets for my car keys.

'But I did not think anything serious would happen. I just wanted someone to find my shoe-horns, that's all. Mr Isles said that he would.'

'Esther, you've caused me a great deal of trouble and you must understand that I cannot speak to you – please go away!'

'But I didn't want to get you into trouble – '

'Esther, go away!'

I finally clambered into my car and slammed the door. Ignoring her rappings on the window, I drove quickly away. As I glanced into my rear-view mirror I could see her crying helplessly at the kerbside. I instinctively braked and was greatly tempted to return and see her safely back home. Self-preservation proved too strong, however, and I shook my head and sped out of the street.

On my return home, my wife gave me a message to telephone my chief inspector as soon as possible. What now! I somehow had a gut feeling that Esther might have killed herself. I quickly dialled the station number and was greatly surprised to find him still at his office.

'I'm sorry,' he said, 'but you'll have to do the whole thing again. This complaint should have been investigated by a senior officer from another station. Report to Tower Bridge Police Station on Thursday at 2 pm. The superintendent there will see you. He is now entirely in charge of the investigations, that is, until the papers come back from the Director of Public Prosecutions. Oh, and good luck.'

I replaced the telephone and the worried face of my wife reminded me that she was not yet aware of anything that had transpired.

'But what will happen? What will they do to you?' she asked anxiously, after I had recited the whole story to her.

'Well, the criminal allegations are ridiculous. I'm not even worried about them. The discipline aspect is a bit different though. I *did* accept the keys, she *has* made allegations and she *does* live on my patch! She is also a female, and that in itself can be dynamite. I'm only too pleased that she is seventy-four, God only knows what they would have made of it if she had been fifty years younger! I think at the end of the day I'll probably be transferred to another station.'

'Where?'

'How the hell do I know? It's months away yet. It's just something that I'll have to prepare myself for. Anyway,' I added, in a blatant attempt to lighten her gloom, 'half of the bloody station would like a transfer. This'll simply put me ahead of everyone, that's all.'

She did not look at all convinced.

Tower Bridge Police Station is even grimier than Wharf Road. A dirty London drizzle misted its way along the river valley, soaking everything in its path. I climbed the stairs to the superintendent's office and immediately sensed his resentment. To this man I was a nuisance. I was another addition to his work-load. What he would really have liked was a nice tidy 'plea of guilty'. We could then have got it all over and done with. His questioning was particularly aggressive but I was far too sure of my position to become flustered. I did not even worry when he read out to me the official caution. I knew exactly where my battleground would lie. It would revolve entirely around those wretched keys.

The highlight of the interview was the presentation to me of the form 163. This is a form that lays out the entire complaint against the accused officer. It included both the theft allegation and the discipline offence. It must always be served on any policeman before any action is taken against him. My 'crimes' against Esther were neatly listed.

That you did violate Mrs Esther Violet Wood's trust in you by the following measures:

    a)    Use her electric power (i.e. light and fire) while she was away and without her permission.

    b)    Remove from her premises a small quantity of coffee.

    c)    Cause what appeared to be a stain on a small table.

    d)    Interfere with her provisions. The complainant alleges that some minor items in her larder had been replaced in slightly different positions.

    e)    Remove from her premises four envelopes.

f)   Remove a quantity of cosmetic creams from two
    sachets in the bathroom.
g)   Cause the removal of two shoe-horns.

I read carefully through each of the allegations and decided
not to be either facetious or cynical about any of them.
Ludicrous and even bizarre they may have seemed to me;
nevertheless my whole future could easily revolve around
them.

I then signed my written statement and left the room.

I must confess I was totally annihilated by my colleagues.
Every day they seemed to work out a different scenario for
the wild coffee-drinking evening that must have taken place.
The only trouble was, I never found any of them very funny.

Four months almost to the day, I was again summoned to
my chief inspector's office. His greeting this time was
genuinely warm. 'Although I was not in a position to
investigate the complaint against you, I am now in a position
to tell you some good news. The Director of Public Prosecutions has recommended that no action should be taken
against you, over the allegation of theft. The question of
discipline, however, has still to be resolved.' I thanked him,
this time intentionally. That verdict had removed the pre-
liminary; now for the main event.

Later that evening I wandered around to the Community
Development Project. There I chatted with a couple of the
workers who were preparing for an evening advice surgery.

'Look,' said one of them. 'We have heard from quite a
number of local people that they would like to form a deputation to speak to your area commander.'

'Whatever for?' I asked, peering at them over the top of a
chipped Arsenal Football Club mug.

'They seemed to feel that they could speak out against

119

Councillor Isles in a way that you would never be able to.'

'No!'

'Why not?'

'Because if I was the commander and you approached me, I would assume that the man under investigation must have drummed up the support himself. I would quite simply feel that something must have been hidden from me. I am very touched by the idea but no, please don't. I feel that it would only aggravate the situation. I am reasonably confident that I can fight this one myself. Thank you. And incidentally,' I added, trying to change the subject, 'my tea-bag's burst.'

'You're a fool and you are casting a slur on the people who are prepared to form a deputation if you think for a moment that they could be manipulated in that fashion. We are speaking of head-teachers, vicars and at least one community leader!'

'I am very grateful, please don't think that I'm not, but I do not want these people to fight my battle for me. That's all there is to it.' I drained my cup, busted tea-bag as well, and sulked my way out of the shop.

I thought little about that conversation until a week later. I was yet again summoned back to the station, this time to see my own superintendent.

'Take a seat, Harry,' was a most promising opening remark. This invited contrast between sitting and standing also signalled the difference between staying and going! 'I've got a great result for you! The commander has told me that you are to stay on your own beat but he begs you, please, please do not accept any more bloody keys! Don't you think that's very fair of him?'

'Yes, but − well, what's happened to the discipline hearing?'

'Why? Do you want one?'

'Well, no, but, well, I just can't work out what's happened!'

'A deputation of local people went to see him, that's all. He was over the moon about it. He's very much in favour of community policing and when he finds that a copper who is in trouble has part of that community turning out to defend him, well, he's bloody delighted!'

'Well, yes,' I said, ungratefully. 'But supposing that I hadn't been a community cop, what then? A transfer to the Isle of Dogs and a six-months traffic point, I reckon!'

'Yeh,' murmured the superintendent, rubbing his chin thoughtfully. 'Yeh, I reckon that would be about it. It's not too late now, though. Would you like one?' I thanked him and graciously declined his offer. 'Okay, off you go,' he ordered, in a surprisingly sympathetic voice. I had reached the door on my way out, when he looked up from his papers and called quite casually to me.

'Sir?' I acknowledged, pausing with my fingers already closed around the door-handle.

'You won't forget about the keys, will you?'

'Never, sir, never in my whole life, I won't.'

## Day of Action

The storm-swept park looked extremely inhospitable. Autumn had blown in over the north-west fence and was feeling its way around the flower garden. True, the trees were still in possession of most of their leaves but they hung very wet and looked ominously tired. 'Jogger's Trail' read the drunkenly nailed sign. It arrowed a path up the gentle slope that led to the boating pool. At least, it had *seemed* gentle on the first time around, but now, on the third circuit, it was looking like the north face of the Eiger. I gritted my teeth and plodded angrily on. I was still smarting from my family's criticism of my fitness.

'You are definitely thickening around the waist and you're looking more unfit each day.' This was bad enough, but when it had been compounded by '*And* you're drinking too much!' I had gone on a determined search for my track-suit and trainers. Well, I could certainly have picked a better day. The storms that queued to batter south-east London all seemed to have eyed-in on Forster Park. I had no set plan to regain my fitness but as a follow-up to my jogging, I had intended cycling to work the following day.

Wednesday dawned bright and clear. The previous day's storms had vanished, leaving just the leaves and bent-over dahlias to indicate that they had ever been here at all. It was some twenty years since I had cycled the nine miles to work, so today would be an adventure. The few aches that remained from my Forster Park jog simply hardened my resolve to ignore them. I would sweep gracefully and silently into the station yard – well, perhaps I might *just* ring my bell – as I ignored the pain barrier. With any luck I could be in the pink of condition by the weekend.

My early enthusiasm wore off at the first hill. By the time I 'swung into the station yard', my legs no longer belonged to me, my eyes watered incessantly and my bum was on fire. I parked the lone cycle among the forty or so motor-bikes of my colleagues and walked bow-leggedly across the yard. 'I'll never recover!' I thought. What a terrible thing is middle age! I was desperately trying to devise a scheme for the day that would result in my sitting down for the maximum amount of time. This was not going to be easy. I had been due to start work at 8 am. However, because I had run out of steam eight miles ahead of schedule, I was now at least half an hour late. Before I did anything, I needed to freshen up. I was bent low over the wash-basin when a young PC entered the toilet. While he stood facing the porcelain, he proceeded to pass the time of day with me.

'You look knackered!' was his warm, opening remark.

As a general rule, all nineteen-year-old policemen think that anyone over thirty-five 'looks knackered', so I was not as distressed as I might have been.

'Hey!' he went on. 'Everyone was looking for you about half an hour ago.'

'Yes, I know, I'm a bit late.'

'No, it wasn't for that, they wanted you for something else. Now, what was it?' He paused and looked for inspiration up the flush tank. 'I remember.' He turned towards me and zippered up. 'Trevor's gone sick and you've taken his place on the TUC "Day of Action" march.'

'What! What's Trevor gone sick with?'

123

'He played rugby yesterday in new boots and he's got a badly blistered heel.'

'Oh, so poor Trevor's got a badly blistered heel, has he? Do you know that both my lungs have collapsed and my arse is on fire? Do you know that?' I must say that he showed not the slightest surprise at my news. Perhaps I really did look as bad as he claimed.

I raced up to the front office just as quickly as my twin ailments would allow.

'Ah ha!' called the station officer. 'You're just the bloke. Quick, hurry up, there's a coach outside. Trevor's gone sick and you're in his place!'

'Sod Trevor!' I was about to extend that viewpoint into a whole list of excuses as to just why I could not escort this trade union march when I realized that I was too tired even to argue!

The cheers that are reserved for late-comers on an outing such as this rang out as I entered the coach. Twenty-three of my colleagues were already scattered in positions throughout the fifty-six-seater vehicle. Well, at least there was plenty of room. I fould myself a twin seat and spread out. With any luck we would be on reserve and I might even snatch some sleep.

First I needed to find out exactly what we were supposed to be doing. The inspector in charge of our group was a comparatively young man who had just completed a year as an instructor at the police training school. He was also new to me. These two facts placed me instinctively on the defensive. I was, after all, half an hour late and usually these types were far more authoritative than their more street-weary fellow inspectors. I was agreeably surprised. He had a good open face and a pleasant sense of humour. Even more important, he never once mentioned my time-keeping.

'What're we doing, guv?' I asked.

'We are going straight to Battersea Park for a meal. Then we are going to the South Bank. The marchers will assemble there and we should move off around midday,' he explained.

'Are we, er, walking?' I could hardly bring myself to mention the word.

'Yes. All the way. We'll pick up the march as it leaves the South Bank and we'll escort it throughout the West End to Reformer's Tree in Hyde Park.' I groaned. 'We'll be on our way just as soon as the prison bus goes past us,' he added, ignoring my misery.

This last reference related to the large single-decker bus that calls daily at all police stations to pick up overnight prisoners and convey them to the local magistrates' court. It was at that moment trying to squeeze by. Wharf Road Police Station is situated in a narrow cul-de-sac. It is an extremely busy station and there is regularly a problem with parked cars and other vehicles that require urgent access. Today was one such day. With our fifty-six-seater coach already in the street, there was very little room for the bus to manoeuvre. In fact the total space between the two vehicles measured six inches, which would have been fine – if we had not had a nine-inch mirror. The grating sound set my teeth on edge and the coach driver was not at all amused. The explanation of the bus driver – 'If ye hadna ha' had a mirror, I'd'a' got past' – did precious little to soothe.

After the statutory pause for the exchange of particulars, we were on our way. Traffic was very heavy: the protest march had been well publicized and many commuters had used their cars rather than risk the uncertainties of public transport. The predictable result was that all public transport ran normally. The traffic volume therefore was about

125

forty per cent up on normal, with probably fewer people travelling to work!

Our journey to Battersea Park took us against the flow of town-bound traffic and our driver was greatly relieved. 'Can't stand all that traffic meself, sends me potty,' he pronounced. It struck me that any coach driver who had a tendency to be 'sent potty' in heavy traffic definitely bore watching. I made a mental note before I fell asleep.

I was rudely awoken from my early slumber by a cry from one of the sergeants.

'Stop, sir! We're twenty-three blokes short!'

'What!' responded our inspector in panic disbelief.

The sergeant had been idly perusing the day's operation orders and discovered that we should have called into Southwark Police Station on the way to collect another inspector, two more sergeants and twenty extra PCs. I swore vehemently – bang goes my kip on a double seat.

'Stop, driver, stop!'

We had been just about to enter the notorious Vauxhall one-way system. Once inside, we would have been doomed for the next thirty minutes; it was like a river of no return. The driver cursed again. We were two-thirds of the way to Battersea and now he had to turn around and return to Southwark. Even worse, the crawling traffic that we had so gleefully passed going in the opposite direction was now all anchored, bumper-to-bumper, ahead of us.

'You don't think that it is going to be one of those days?' I asked the driver, sympathetically.

He did not answer me directly but said angrily to no one in particular, 'Every time I look in this splintered mirror, I see eighty-seven bloody motor-cyclists!'

We reluctantly joined the slow-moving queue back to Southwark. It was over an hour later before we had picked up our full complement and driven once again the three mad-dening miles to Battersea.

Battersea Park on a beautiful September morning really takes some beating. On such a day it is one of London's loveliest parks. It was now ten o'clock and the sun had chased away the early autumn mists. Well, not quite all. Wispy little pockets of it lay sleeping in occasional hollows. A very faint trace still hung over the lake. With the leaves just tinged with brown, all the scene lacked was a tall nude inserting one toe in the waterside shallows. Sadly there was no nude – just a fisherman in waders. He may have kept as still, but he didn't look as good.

Our coach made a three-quarter circuit of the park before we came to the Metropolitan Police enclosure. It was like tent city. Huge marquees and smaller tents abounded. We joined the score of other coaches from districts all over London. Nearly half of the Metropolitan force would be fed here today. The inspector whom we had picked up from Southwark had little of the ease that our own man had. He seemed permanently conscious of his rank. Every few minutes he would call out additional commands – and we had yet to alight from the coach! These orders were often no more than commonsense suggestions, yet he made them sound like royal decrees. It is strange how some men command simply with their presence, and others only with their authority.

'Right, pay attention! When you get off this coach, you will enter the marquee by that entrance there.' He pointed to a large extended covered entrance. 'Once inside the mar-quee, you will remain together. I do not want men wandering about aimlessly all over the park. You will get your breakfast and sit at the tables provided and then, when you have finished, I want you to assemble outside. After that

127

it's all straight back on the coach. Is that clear?'

'Is he always like this?' whispered a young Wharf Road PC to his Southwark counterpart.

'No, usually he's far worse,' came the bored reply.

Having listened to the lesson in total disbelief, I alighted with the rest of my colleagues and made for the marquee. On entering, we were delighted to find a white-tape barrier running down the centre of the gangway. Half of the men were obviously expected to go to the left, the remainder to the right. The result of this dilution was that each group then went in opposite directions and sat down to their breakfast in two totally different marquees. In addition, the exits from these marquees would take us even further apart. We took a fiendish delight in this. Less than one minute after the 'You-will-remain-together' sermon, we were scattered to all four corners of the complex. I was additionally happy when I realized that our führer was the first bloke we had lost!

These mealtimes can be quite social occasions. It is possible to meet friends and acquaintances from all over London, many of whom one has not seen for years. I usually like to sit and just take stock of the ages and appearances of some of the younger officers, of both sexes. While I was involved in this activity, a piercing scream cut through the marquee, followed by gales of laughter. The reason for the hysteria was nothing more sinister than an old-fashioned daddy-long-legs. One such insect had apparently alighted on the shoulder of a pretty young WPC and she promptly screamed the place down! The irony caused me to smile. During her police career she will probably deal with arson, rapes and robberies; accidents, buggeries and break-ins. She will search smelly drunks, comfort lousy kids and walk lonely streets. But she is never going to be much use with spiders!

Some thirty minutes later and without too much searching,

we all climbed aboard our coach. I took a final look at the lake — sadly, there was still no nude — and we moved slowly away to the South Bank.

The South Bank is the area that lies between Westminster and Waterloo bridges on the south side of the Thames. There, in a large car park and gardens, the marchers were to assemble. As our coach made its way through the arriving crowds, everywhere there appeared confusion. Friends who had arranged to meet each other had simply not envisaged the volume of people who would be present. Many had planned to return home together after the march, and while some had the money, others would have the tickets. An air of desperation hung over these lost groups as they ran to and fro in a frantic search. There must have been somewhere around 70,000 people milling around. A few appeared to know exactly what was expected of them but the majority just looked bewildered.

The police were by no means exempt from this uncertainty. As the temperature began to climb, so the lower ranks had their usual battle over the wearing of 'shirt-sleeve order': we took our jackets off, 'they' told us to put them back on again. I can never understand how a person who is expected to deal with any situation that may arise in the streets has to be told when he needs to wear a jacket! Having put our tunics back on, we were told our escort position would be near the front of the march.

A steward with a loud-hailer then began to coax and cajole the crowd, with astonishing success, into something approaching a recognizable body. Very slowly, the huge mass began to take shape. Somewhere a band began to play and the front of the procession shuffled slowly forward, like a disintegrating glacier. Late-comers continued to run in all directions in efforts to find their marching friends.

'This is a bit of a mess, guv'nor, isn't it?' I asked a passing chief superintendent.

'This?' he responded cheerfully. 'Lord, no, it's bloody marvellous! You should see the CND – they don't have a clue!'

We made steady progress until we reached the centre of Westminster Bridge where for some reason we stopped. The best place to be on any great march is near the front. Every falter, every spurt is accentuated threefold near the back. I took the opportunity during the pause to look down the river, back towards our starting place at the South Bank. I could see thousands of people who had still to join the march. This was truly the greatest procession that I had ever witnessed.

The purpose of the march was, as I understood it, to show solidarity with the pay claim of the health workers. Yet there appeared to be a great range of other quite strange causes put forward. One huge banner read: 'A Living Wage for Nurses *and* Give Back Diego Garcia!'

One problem for any copper on a march is the lack of originality in most chants. 'Maggie! Maggie! Maggie! – Out! Out! Out!' is all very well for the first hour, but after that it does begin to pale a little. I therefore found it a welcome change of tempo to see several nurses lining up in a conga formation. With their hands on the hips of the person in front of them, they sang out loudly to the conga rhythm:

> Mag-gie-has-not-got-one,
> Nor-man-Fow-ler-is-one,
> Ay-Ay-Ay, Ay-Ay-Ay.

Hundreds of Japanese tourists seemed to think that the whole operation was staged just for them, like the Changing of the Guard, or Beating the Retreat. They stood three-deep, smiling benignly and waving their little union jacks. I think they expected to see the Queen halfway down the procession waving back to them from a howdah. In addition to their union jacks, each of the tourists sported dozens of stick-on protest labels. These little round stickers were attached to everything and everyone – including policemen. For the first time in my recollection, coppers did not seem to object. Perhaps their attitudes could be found in the comment of one of them: 'All of our blokes here today are on their best behaviour. They've got to be, half of their bloody wives are on the march!'

This traditional police-nurse relationship was not without its disadvantages. One young nurse had seen fit to bring her small son along. The child, who rejoiced in the name of Thurston, was three years old and an utter brat. He never ceased moaning and complaining. While I omitted to discover what category of nurse his mother was, she was most definitely not dental. That kid never stopped eating. He devoured sweets by the score, plus two sticky buns and an orange. He was, to my undying shame, the son of a policeman. Thurston had spent most of the march being pushed along in a small folding baby-buggy. There were a few other children in similar circumstances but he was the only one consistently to grizzle. All the other kids seemed to enjoy themselves greatly.

'I wanna carry!' was his repetitive catch-phrase. I think that child prefaced just about everything he said with those first two words. 'You wanna wallop, mate, that's what you want!' was my instinctive reaction. Daphne, Thurston's rather amply built mother, regaled me for most of the early journey with hair-raising tales of her husband's valiant constabulary adventures. By the time the procession had reached Parliament Square, I had had Thurston, Daphne and the absent husband Eldon just about up to my eyebrows.

I slowed my step a little and moved some twenty yards back down the march. I soon found myself walking alongside a pleasant-faced, middle-aged ancillary worker. We began to make easy conversation as we ambled along side by side, and kept talking for most of the length of Whitehall. Eventually our deliberations were interrupted by a chorus of shouts from her colleagues.

'Hey, Gwyneth! You're not here to flirt with the coppers! C'mon and sing!'

'I can't,' answered the embarrassed Gwyneth. 'Every time I do my top-set falls down.'

I closed my eyes sadly. That's bloody middle age again. The first bird that I've pulled for ages and her teeth are falling out!

Scores of people had, like Gwyneth's teeth, fallen out long before we reached the halfway stage. The stop-start flow of the procession was now constantly changing, and by the time we had reached Piccadilly I had two charming new companions. These were two nurses from Swansea. They sidled seductively up and asked if I knew the location of the nearest toilets. I told them that the most accessible one would be at Hyde Park Corner. Once there, they could run ahead of the march and rejoin us as we were passing. I added that at the rate we were travelling, we should be there in about ten minutes. They looked doubtfully at one another but eventually agreed to attempt it. Unfortunately for the two girls, we seemed to experience more hold-ups in Piccadilly than on any other part of the route. This ten minutes evolved painfully into three-quarters of an hour, by which time the nurses were looking decidedly uncomfortable.

'Just a few minutes more,' I encouraged. 'We're almost there!' My two new acquaintances were by this time practically knock-kneed. 'Hold on! Look, there it is!' I pointed to the entrance that led below the pavement some hundred yards ahead.

Without more ado, they dropped their 'Fair Pay for Nurses' banner and scuttled crouchingly away to the accompaniment of great cheers from their colleagues. Thirty seconds later they emerged from the toilet steps, agony showing in their every move. The lavatory attendant had nobly decided to show solidarity with their claim – she had therefore closed the place for two hours! Desperate situations call for desperate measures. I therefore had a quick word with the driver of a stationary police van, and the last time that I saw either of the nurses they were disappearing behind it.

We were now only some half-mile from the finishing line and I could see Daphne and Thurston still slightly ahead of me. The child's bottom lip was in its perpetual state of quiver as he grizzled his way along Park Lane. Suddenly Daphne staggered, and only the straps of the baby-buggy stopped Thurston from being pitched into the road. The buggy fell on to its side and the small section of the procession immediately around them came to a stop. One of the buggy wheels had broken and, in an attempt to balance it, Daphne had lost the heel of her left shoe.

The boy was naturally quite frightened by this turn of events. He doubtless felt that he now had an opportunity to fret with every justification. Thurston was not a child to let such an opportunity pass, and he really let rip. Several brave colleagues of Daphne gallantly offered to carry the screaming child for the remaining distance. Thurston, however, was having none of it. Daphne had managed to fold up the buggy and the march was now moving forward again, this time around her. The poor girl had been directed by one of the stewards to leave the march and cut across the park to the finishing line, a saving in distance of some six hundred yards. I impulsively decided to make a token gesture. After all, I felt that I had some affinity with the girl.

'I'll carry it for you if you wish,' I offered. 'It's only a short distance now and I'll manage it all right,' I added modestly. I stretched out my hands to relieve her of the three-wheeled buggy.

'Oh, Thurston, did you hear that? The policeman will carry you for the rest of the way. He's just like daddy!'

'No – well,' I began.

But it was no use. Daphne's group were now some distance ahead. She was surrounded by strangers, sympathetic no doubt, but strangers nevertheless.

'Come on, then!' I growled at the boy, still not thinking that he would respond. To my astonishment he came like a lamb. There were no screaming fits, no grizzles, no 'wannas' – just a sticky, smelly, tearful bundle of abject misery. I made a weak attempt at conversation but this was handicapped by my inability to speak about his dad. It was something that I could just not bring myself to do. Although I had not met his father Eldon, I instinctively hated the man and I was sure it would show.

'How about football, Thurston, you like football, I bet!'

'No, I don't!' he snapped.

I was then finished. I find it impossible to talk to any kid who doesn't like football. We finished the march in total silence, except, that is, for his occasional sobs. We crossed the line looking like a Flanders stretcher party. My own limbs were now bitterly complaining about jogging, cycling, marching and Thurston. My helmet was at a silly angle and I was far too tired to right it. Thurston was beginning to smell of other aromas beside oranges. Daphne had removed her left shoe and her gait had all of the fluency of a marcher with a wooden leg.

'Here y'are, luv,' I said, as I dropped the now ripening Thurston into her plump arms.

'Thanks, my lovely. I'll tell Eldon when I get back home. He'll probably write to you.'

I crossed my fingers. 'Please don't ask for my address,' I prayed.

Daphne doubtless had far too much on her plate to give that a thought. Bidding me goodbye, she dragged the boy behind her and went wearily into the crowd in search of her companions. 'Say tat-ta, Thurston,' she called over her shoulder.

Thurston sniffed twice in rapid succession and said nothing.

As the marchers streamed into the park, more and more nurses slipped away in desperate search of a toilet. I think that when I leave the police force I will open a mobile lavatory for demonstrators. Soon the main body of the march had left the road and spilled out on to the grass. All banners were handed in to the organizers and most marchers just slipped quietly to the ground.

With a good eye for business, an ice-cream vendor had parked just across the road between the crowd and our police coach. He had been there for only a few minutes when a police motor-cyclist arrived and ordered him away. Although the queues of expectant buyers did not seem too distressed by this action, loud boos came from the direction of the police coaches. Unfortunately, the battery of the ice-cream van appeared defective and the driver was unable to start the engine. Every copper in the coaches decided that it was now a good time to look the other way. The poor traffic cop then had no alternative but to put his shoulder to

135

the rear and heave. The van slowly gathered momentum and obliterated the pusher in a cloud of blue smoke.

Our coach was by this time parked conveniently close by and we thankfully climbed aboard. Some of us watched with great interest as the last of the marchers arrived, others fell instantly asleep. Soon our radio informed us of our dismissal. The next saga would be for the driver to negotiate the West End traffic. It was now in an appalling state. By the time we arrived back at Wharf Road Police Station an hour or so later, my legs had seized up through sitting for too long. I quickly changed out of uniform and wearily made my way to the cycle shed.

'Where's yer car, Harry?' said an enquiring colleague.

'My car? Well, I, er, left it at home as an experiment.'

'An experiment?'

'Yes, an experiment to get fit.'

'Oh, that's okay then, only I was going to offer you a lift.'

'A lift! You're on! You wouldn't care for a pint on the way home, would you?'

## The Great Garage Search

Old May shuffled busily along the Walworth Road pavement. She was very much a local character with her threadbare slippers and her long black frock. I noticed that she was now using an old walking stick, and this saddened me greatly. May was a lady who spent a great deal of time just wandering the local streets. She was a harmless and determined eccentric. Unfortunately, she was also frail and vulnerable. This combination had been too much of a temptation for two strapping fifteen-year-old youths. They had pounded her into the gutter and made off with her handbag. May had sustained a bad pelvic fracture in the attack, hence the stick. However the experience had not daunted her in the slightest. Rain or shine, night or day, she could usually be seen toing and froing from her flat to God knows where.

I had not seen her for some time and felt quite guilty about this omission. I was always reluctant to call on her at home because, well, it was a little ripe there, to say the least. The alternative was to meet her in the streets. This also presented a problem. One really needed a good thirty minutes to have any conversation with May and usually I could not spare that sort of time. Well, today I could. I climbed down from my cycle and crossed the road with genuine pleasure both to meet her – and to placate my conscience.

'Hullo, May, luv, how are you?

''Ullo 'Arry, mate! Hi'm fine, really.' She had a habit of

137

never sounding the letter 'H' except in the wrong place.

'How's the new flat?' I knew I was taking a chance mentioning this, because she hated it. She had been moved out of her old, damp, top-floor tenement flat into a beautiful new ground-floor maisonette. Her old street was slowly being vacated, ready for the demolition crew's great steam-hammer.

May had always been something of a 'street-raker' but since her change of accommodation she had been much worse. Most of her street-wanderings were little more than nostalgic missions to her old flats. There she would sit against the bonnet of any conveniently parked car and relive her girlhood. The old tenements were spread over six narrow streets and many families still remained in them. This all helped to draw her back. Deep down, I think she was secretly hoping that by some miracle she might yet be re-offered her old flat again. Fairly soon the entire block would be razed to the ground, then she would probably adjust — providing, of course, that she lived that long. No one knew just how old May was, but her health, particularly since the mugging, was fading fast.

'Hit's bleedin' 'orrible, 'Arry. What wiv the kids an' everyfing — well, yer just carn't git a moment's peace, can yer?'

'No, May,' I answered, sympathetically, assuming that was what she wanted me to say.

'Hi tell yer what Hi fink his wrong, though.'

'What's that, May?'

'Well, Hi fink that hit's wrong that they are gonna blow up the old buildin's.'

'What old buildings?'

'My old buildin's, a' course — Pullen's Buildin's!'

'No, they are not, May. They wouldn't blow them up! They will just knock them down, a block at a time.'

'Well, if they can't blow 'em up, then why 'ave they put a bomb in 'em? Go on, tell me that, eh? Why 'ave they?'

'May,' I said patiently, 'they are not going to blow up Pullen's Buildings, I promise you. Who told you there's a bomb there?'

'Hi've seen hit.'

'Where?'

'Hin Crampton Street!'

'All right, then, May. I'll tell you what I'll do. I'll come with you to Crampton Street and you show me where the bomb is, all right? If it's there, I'll take it away. How's that?'

'Hall right, Hi'll show you exactly, right now!'

'Fine!'

It took longer to reach Crampton Street than I expected. May's physical condition had deteriorated much more than I had realized. Our quarter-mile journey was regularly punctuated by short stops for a rest. We finally entered the street and she pointed vaguely to a position halfway down on the west side.

'Hit's dahn there, underneaf a big blue van!'

'All right, May, now I know where it is, I'll go on ahead and you catch me up, all right?'

I increased my pace and was soon alongside a tatty old blue Ford transit van. The tyres were soft and the windscreen shattered. Rust, dust and pigeon droppings covered the whole vehicle. The street cleaners had meticulously swept around it and the dirt of months lay beneath it. A couple of old tyres were inside, together with a pile of filthy coats and a few empty meth' bottles. I crouched down on the pavement and looked underneath. Suddenly my heart gave a thump and my bum twitched sharply. There, lying in a clean white plastic bag, was a small bundle. At least three, possibly five, tubular objects were inside the bag, and a small length of red

139

wire extended from its opening. Surely not a bomb?

'There y'are, 'Arry, mate, Hi told yer, didn't Hi? Hit's a bomb, hain't hit?'

'Well, I don't know about that, May. I tell you what. You go home and I'll come around and see you later on. It can't be a bomb, now can it?' I said in an attempt to reassure her. 'I mean, who would want to blow up Crampton Street?'

'Well, the sanitary hinspector might, for a start. But okay, 'Arry, mate, don't blow yer bleedin' self hup, though, will yer? Tat-ta!' With that, she tapped her way back down the street and was lost from my sight.

I now had a problem. Our instructions were quite clear on the subject of suspect parcels. We were to contact the station then remove the batteries from our radios. These batteries, it was believed, could sometimes trigger off an explosive device. The station in turn then contacts our duty officer and, in the last resort, the bomb disposal squad. There are no laurels awarded to anyone who tackles a package, however straightforward, on his own. Nor is any criticism made of a copper who calls out the squad on a false alarm.

In spite of these directions, it is inevitable that occasionally a PC has to make a decision for himself. I was now faced with that decision. Contrary to old May's suspicions, who on earth would want to blow up a dosser's truck and half of Pullen's Buildings? It just did not make sense. Unfortunately, bombs and explosive devices rarely do make sense. Only a few days earlier there had been a series of explosions in the West End, including one in a dustbin. It is just as illogical to detonate a dustbin as it is to blow up a dosser.

I walked to the corner of the street and called the station on my bat-phone. I told them that I did not *think* it was a bomb but I was about to have a closer look at it and I would call them back. 'Okay, but don't forget to remove your battery before you examine the parcel,' came the predictable response.

This reminder had a particular significance: just the week before, a recruit had also found a suspect package. He correctly called for the duty officer, who had arrived within minutes. 'Go and take out your battery, lad, while I examine the package.' A few seconds later, the inspector's attention was drawn by the young constable standing over him. He was then offered the still intact radio. 'Excuse me, sir, – I can't get the thing out!'

Well I most certainly was going to get the 'thing out' before I spent any more time examining that bag. I unhooked radio and battery from my belt and hung them over the handle-bars of my cycle. Seconds later, I resumed my crouch alongside the van. I found that the only way I could gain access to the package was by lying on the kerbstones at the pavement edge. I removed my helmet and, with my head partially under the vehicle, reached out to the 'bomb'. Whatever the contents were, they were much smaller than the bag itself. It occurred to me that if I could cut or tear the plastic very carefully, I would be able to see inside. What I needed was a very sharp knife or, even better, a razor blade.

I gingerly removed my head and arms while I considered the next step. Perhaps someone in Pullen's Buildings would be able to help. I decided to knock on a few doors. As I pulled myself to my feet, I instinctively looked up. There were four storeys of windows above me and nearly every one of them contained a head! If the dosser's truck was indeed a bomb, the effect would be like a giant coconut-shy! Unmarked torsos would slip headlessly to the floor as their departed skulls rained down into the street. I could just imagine their mass greeting by St Peter – 'I've invited you all here today – because you are all bloody nosey!'

141

'Will you go in?' I yelled. 'Or at least come down here and undo the sodding thing yourself!'

I was amazed at their reluctance to comply. Some seemed to think that if they only peeped with one eye over the window sill, it wouldn't count. Others pulled their heads in a little and leaned backwards, at the same time looking sharply down their noses. One fellow at ground level was breathtaking. He was easily the most vulnerable, being just four feet away. He had closed his windows tight-shut and stood confidently looking at me through the glass! He probably thought it was television.

'Have you got a razor?' I mouthed.

He appeared taken aback at this. I think he expected computers, remote-control or at least something from *Star Wars*. Instead he had me, my bike and a demented request for a razor. However, he gave an understanding nod, so I moved towards his front door to meet him. After a few seconds I heard him slip the bolt. The door opened to reveal a slim middle-aged moustached man. He eagerly offered me a shiny bright Remington Super-Sixty electric razor!

'No! I want a *blade,* guv'nor! Haven't you got a sodding blade?' I asked irritably.

'Oh, I'm sorry. I thought you had some secret means of . . .'

'Look! Have you got a razor blade or haven't you? It is bloody urgent!'

'My wife has – she uses it for her legs!'

I was very tempted to say that I wouldn't really care if she used it for her haemorrhoids. All I wanted was a blade, and quick!

Within a few seconds he had given me a whole packet. I approached the bag again and the sharp edge sliced easily through the plastic cover, completely revealing our 'bomb'. It

142

was nothing more sinister than a bag of bathroom refuse. It contained an empty shampoo bottle, two toilet-roll rollers, a talc tin and a box of bath salts that had solidified in the dampness of Pullen's Buildings. The 'wire' was in fact a length of red string that had obviously been attached to the salts when they were purchased, presumably as a present.

Leaving the bag where it was, I returned the blades to their owner and fervently hoped that no one had nicked either my bike or my radio. I just did not feel in the mood to tell May about her bomb. In any case, she would only have been disappointed. The heads had by this time all resumed their places at the windows. I glared up but resisted the temptation to shout 'bang' loudly.

All over London there had been scores of false alarms similar to this one. There had also been many incidents of the real thing. It was the run-in to Christmas and therefore a traditional time for terrorists to take off other people's arms and legs.

A new approach to combat this threat had been worked out by Scotland Yard's anti-terrorist squad. Every policeman was required to attend a briefing. There they were told that starting on the following Monday, it was intended to list and search every lock-up garage in the Greater London area. The project was a massive one. It would make such a colossal demand on manpower that I could not see how it could be accomplished. I honestly believed, right up until the time that we left the station to begin the first search, that the whole idea was nothing more than a gigantic bluff. I was appalled when I discovered that it was for real.

We were split into teams, usually of three constables plus a sergeant. We were allocated an area and we had to produce results. Either there were explosives in the garage or there weren't, but every single garage had to be searched. Every garage-owner and its tenant was listed, together with the registration number of any vehicle therein, and the time was noted. Great play was made of the lists of tenants provided to us by the council. 'You'll find these lists invaluable,' we were told at the briefing. 'They will cut your leg-work by half.' In the main they were quite useless. They were sometimes as much as ten years out of date. In fact the main accomplishment of this search was to reveal the chaotic state of council records. Thousands upon thousands of pounds must be lost each year on garage rents alone.

A system of searching an area was suggested, but most coppers improvised – usually disastrously. The search overran by weeks. I have never heard PCs complain quite so much as they did during this exercise. It was easily the most tedious, time-consuming and frustrating job that I have ever been involved in. We worked from seven in the morning to nine at night, reducing to twelve hours a day after the first week. A random check on any ten constables would be fortunate to find more than one with a torch that worked. Therefore many of the searches were carried out in the dark. The weather was dreadful: the only time that it ceased to rain was when it snowed. The ink on the clipboards ran, and within twenty minutes of the start of the day's search everyone would be absolutely filthy.

Most of the lock-up garages on the Wharf Road manor are underground. Our patch is littered with huge housing estates, and since the late 1960s, the policy has been to insert great rows of garages beneath them. The problem with garages on council estates is that while people may move house, they do not always move garage. For example, a garage tenant may have transferred to an estate some distance away, yet still continue to use his old lock-up. One man whom I finally traced, using the determination usually reserved for child-

144

molesters, had moved up the social scale to the stockbroker belt at Woking, some twenty-five miles away. He daily drove to London and simply used his old garage as a regular car park. He had not even been a council tenant for four years!

Many of these lock-ups were empty (particularly those which council records listed as occupied). However it was very difficult to confirm these vacancies without first opening the door. The problem then arose – how to gain access, without force, to locked premises that have no owner?

A colleague had an inspired idea. He went along to a well-known thieving teenager and 'leaned' on him a little. The lad helpfully explained to him a very simple means of entry. With a box to stand on, a torch to see with and a piece of stiff wire to wiggle, access could be gained to upwards of a dozen garages in two minutes flat.

If the ordinary street copper was not endeared to this mammoth search, the criminal fraternity cared for it even less. It was alleged that once the searching had ceased for the day, usually around 9 pm, many estates would suddenly burst into life. Great numbers of shadowy figures would scarper ant-like in the dark, transferring 'gear' from garages that had yet to be searched into others that had. It availed them little. The searching was so chaotic that some garages were searched five times while others were missed entirely. No system could have been evolved to combat ours. Three hundred car radios, for example, had three changes of garage before they were finally abandoned on the pavement in sheer frustration.

In the main, though, it was not widespread crime that was uncovered, so much as a 'liberal' interpretation of the tenancy agreements. One tenant on an estate near the Elephant and Castle paid £1.50 per week for his new lock-up garage. When I discovered a £15,000 Mercedes snuggled down in there,

I thought it might be interesting to find out why. The tenant explained that his own car, a 1965 Hillman Imp, valued around forty quid, was parked outside in the street. He then re-let his garage to a suburban gentleman during working hours for £50 per month.

Another estate in the same area contained long, narrow garages, enabling some astute tenants to push their own cars right down to the far wall, and still leave ample space behind for a daily commuter. With schemes like these, it wasn't just a case of having your cake and eating it – you could sell it as well!

It was in that particular section of garages that the morale of my own search gang really reached rock-bottom. Our list showed that garage number 176 was empty. But being by now totally disillusioned with all of our council lists, we decided to open it. We wiggled our wire and gained an easy access. Once inside we found an old Austin 1100 saloon pushed tightly against the far wall. A brand new Ford Cortina was slotted equally tightly behind it. Any copper who sees a Ford car in such a situation will immediately assume that it must have been stolen. In fact I would have been convinced it was nicked even if the Pope himself was sitting at the wheel.

'Check the numbers,' said our sergeant, with his pen and clipboard at the ready.

The forty-watt bulb that glowed weakly in the underground driveway did its best but all we could really see was the rear part of the new car. We did not have a torch or match between us.

'I can't see it, sarge!'

'Well, perhaps if one of you works his way down to the back of the 1100 you'll be able to feel the numbers – a bit like braille.'

146

Unfortunately the two cars were not the only articles in the garage. There were numerous boxes, tyres and a general accumulation of unseen rubbish along the walls. I sensibly decided that if there was to be any climbing of obstacles in the dark, that could best be accomplished by my two younger colleagues, Mark and Frank. I therefore joined the sergeant at the door, purely in an advisory capacity. The Cortina was so tightly parked against the front car that they found it impossible to slip their hands between the two vehicles in order to read the plates.

'Well, you'll just have to work your way down to the front plates,' I suggested, authoritatively.

This was far easier said than done. The clatter of boxes and the swearing of oaths emphasized the difficulty that was being experienced out there in the pitch blackness. A grunt and a few groans finally indicated that our Mark was now lying upside down on the bonnet of the Austin. A faint and rapid flicker of light also indicated that Mark had now remembered his cigarette lighter. After about the fifth attempt, it finally lit, but as soon as Mark dropped his head down on the radiator grille, it went out. No amount of flicking could re-kindle it. He then felt down with his hands and called out the number. 'E-Y-K . . . 4-4-3 . . . C' At least that is what it was supposed to have been, but lying upside down in the dark with a mouthful of dust did not make for clarity. However, the second young constable who was balancing, not without some difficulty, between the two cars on the opposite side of the garage, did seem to hear.

'What did he say?' I asked, peering into the dark.

'I think he said KGC 843C,' replied the unseen voice.

I then turned to the sergeant who was standing out in the driveway and much nearer the dim light 'KGC 843C,' I repeated.

147

He nodded in acknowledgement.

After a great deal more clattering, banging and swearing, both men emerged into the sparsely lit driveway. They were absolutely filthy. They spent some minutes brushing each other down with their gloves while I closed the garage door.

Just as we were about to move along to the next garage, the sergeant said to Mark, 'What was the number of that Austin, Mark?'

'Er, I forget now, sarge. KGK 8 something or other, I think it was – but Frank'll know, I told him.'

'Frank,' called the sergeant to the shadowy figure already tampering with the next garage door, 'what was that car number again?'

'KGC 483C, sarge, at least I think it was, but Harry'll know.'

I was saying nothing. I had already forgotten it!

'What was the number of that Austin, Harry?'

'I told you,' I responded, matter-of-factly.

'You may have done,' he answered, just a fraction icily, 'but I never wrote it down. What was it again?'

'I forget!'

We all looked at each other in total disbelief. We had spent fifteen minutes trying to obtain the rotten number. Each of us had repeated it, and now, two minutes later, none of us could remember it!

'This never happens on the television, sarge,' Frank said, rather sadly, I felt.

The publicity that this search received had some strange side-effects. Hardly anyone objected to the search. The complaints came instead from people who had not been searched. It was as if they felt neglected. 'Old Charlie next door has had his garage searched. Can't you search mine?' They not only wished their garage to be searched but they insisted on showing every single item that they had stored there. They opened up boxes, unscrewed tins, lifted up cupboards and unrolled deck-chairs. They would recite the history of their cars and sometimes, if we were particularly unlucky, of their two previous cars. One man even told me at great length about a car that was owned by a bloke whom he once met on holiday. For many the search appeared to be the most exciting thing in their lives for years.

Perhaps the brightest spot for policemen in these searchings was the uncertainty of what one *might* find. I never found any explosives, nor, for that matter, did anyone else from Wharf Road, but there were still some very strange discoveries.

I slipped the catch on one empty exterior garage and lifted up a screechingly hinged up-and-over door. There was a four-inch gap at the bottom of this door and leaves, potato crisp bags and fast-food cartons had all found their way inside. The distant street light gave just enough illumination for me to make out shapes in the interior. At the far end of the garage was a great pile of leaves. Partially buried in them were two stubbly chinned snoring drunks. Scattered all around were empty cheap wine bottles and dozens of wet cigarette stubs. Because of their sleeping innocence, they reminded me at first of the Babes in the Wood. However, on closer scrutiny they certainly did not smell like the babes. I carefully closed the door and tiptoed quietly away.

As the days wore on, more and more officers were returned to their normal duties: day-to-day work was still piling up and refusing to go away. The squads of four were readjusted and different groups were re-formed with the remaining men and women. Because it was policy to keep the community coppers searching until the bitter end, I survived four of these reorganizations. Finally, at the beginning of the

149

third week, we operated singly. We were also instructed that all garage searching had to be completed by the end of that week.

Although there were now comparatively few unsearched lock-ups, those that did remain were obviously the most difficult. This difficulty manifested itself in several ways. Some had absent tenants, others were different in design, therefore our wire did not work. Others had refinements such as additional padlocks or security bolts. There were even some that had been closed for so long that they were like Tutankhamun's tomb, with dirt and weeds solidifying around every crack and join. I therefore could not see how this operation could possibly finish by the end of the week. Together with most of my colleagues, I could see it going on for the rest of the winter!

Each day, as the difficulties escalated, so our clear-up rate was less and less. Finally, on one of our many briefings, a chief inspector told us that any garage that had not been inspected by the end of that week would be forcibly opened.

'How?' we understandably asked.

'With bolt-cutters and, if necessary, sledge-hammers!'

'But how about the security once we have searched them?'

'That's been accounted for. We will replace all of the old locks that we break with brand new ones. The owners will of course be given a new set of keys to go with the lock.'

'Er, while I really do hate to be negative, sir, how do we give the owner these keys if we can't find him in the first place to get into his garage? I mean, if we knew who he was, we wouldn't need to smash open his door!'

'Well, of course, we knew there would be some little difficulties when we began this search, didn't we?' He looked around the group expectantly but received no support from the dead faces. 'But with a little bit of commonsense,' he

150

continued, 'and goodwill on both sides, I'm sure there is nothing that cannot be overcome.'

'Yes, but how do we give him his keys?'

Too late, he'd gone.

I really did have the miseries now. As senior man present, I gave the matter some deep thought and announced my conclusions to a couple of my friends.

'I'm going to the pub.'

'I'll come with you,' said Jim, who had the neighbouring beat.

A few minutes later I pushed open the door of the Duke of Sutherland. This pub is slap-bang in the middle of my patch and some of my outstanding lock-ups were no more than sixty seconds' walk away from it. The click of the saloon bar door has a sound all of its own. This plus the hiss of the ancient gas fire gradually soothed away all nagging thoughts of garages – with, of course, a little help from a couple of pints of best IPA. We were sitting silently staring into our beer when Tom the landlord called across to us.

'What's the matter, lads? You look down tonight.'

'Oh, it's those bloody garages, Tom,' said Jim. 'They seem never-ending.'

As he spoke, I was vaguely aware of a round-faced fellow making his way from the public bar through the small entrance into the saloon side.

'Did you wanna search my garage, Harry?'

Although I did not know his name, I recognized him as a regular from the public bar.

'Where is it?' I asked, with mild interest.

'Over there.' He nodded in the general direction of the dart-board.

'What's the number of it?' My interest was definitely rising.

'282.'

151

'282! I've had that on my list for three weeks and got absolutely nowhere with it! Where the bloody hell have you been?'

'Well, to tell you the truth, it's a bit awkward, like.'

'Why awkward?'

'Well, I'm not really the tenant.'

'Well, I'm not really concerned. All I want to do is to get number 282 off of my bloody list. Who is the tenant, anyway?' I added as an afterthought.

'Well, I s'pose you'd say my dad was. That's if anybody at all was.'

'Where's your dad, then?'

'He's dead.'

'Dead?'

'Died five years ago. I've had the garage ever since.'

'Well, that's no problem. I assume you would have just taken over the tenancy when your father died?'

'Well, no, not really. You see – oh, this is a bit embarrassing – the old man never had the tenancy either.'

'How long did he have the garage for, then?'

'He had it for five years as well.'

'Are you telling me that between the two of you, you've occupied that garage for ten years – and paid no rent!'

'Well, yes, I s'pose that's about the size of it.'

'But those garages are only about ten years old.'

'Yeh, I know.'

'So between you and your dad, you've had that garage rent-free ever since it's been built?'

'Yes. When the estate first went up, the garage was empty. No one seemed to be using it so dad moved in. We've sort of been there ever since.'

'*Sort* of been there ever since!! Bloody hell, I bet you love me, mate, don't you?'

152

'It's not your fault, Harry, it's the bleedin' IRA. They're going to work out bloody expensive for me. Will I have to pay the back rent?'

'Shouldn't think so, but they'll probably work out a new tenancy agreement for you fairly soon, because according to their records it's been empty for ten years.'

'Well, I hope it's not too expensive.'

'If it is you'll have to apply for a rent rebate. Don't ask for it to be retrospective, though, will you?'

'D'you want to look in the garage now?' he said, reaching in his pocket for his keys.

'Come on, then,' I said wearily. 'Just in case *you* drop dead. I don't want to wait for another bloody five years to talk to your son.'

The two of us left the warmth of the pub and stepped out into the dark sleet-streaked air. Within a minute we stood before the reinforced door of garage number 282. The ease of opening indicated that the place was in constant use.

Since my daughter held her eighteenth birthday party in my garage, I have always maintained that I could no longer be surprised at what other people do in theirs – but I was! It was like Aladdin's cave. My companion owned several market stalls and sold a wide diversity of goods. Just about everything seemed to be in there and stacked up to the roof. Blankets, dresses, pots, plates, cups, radios, carpets and dog food!

'Yes, okay,' I sighed, assuming there was nothing in there to go 'bang'. 'Thanks for letting me know.'

'Do you want to see next door as well?'

'D'you mean you have another one?!!!'

'Yes, but I've only had this next one for a year.'

'Oh, that's all right, then!' I said, instinctively raising my eyes. 'Putting it like that, it's barely worth mentioning. Still

153

while we're here it would be a shame not to have a look around, wouldn't it?'

The second lock-up was a duplication of the first.

'Aren't you worried that you may have a break-in?' I asked. 'You must have thousands of pounds' worth of gear here.'

'No, I've got a pretty good alarm system. It ought to be good, it cost me enough!'

I stepped back outside and looked once more at the garages. He had definitely made them extremely solid, and with his particular alarm system they were also reasonably thief-proof. 'Thank's very much, mate – and I'm sorry,' I said, as I gratefully ticked them both from my list.

I returned to the Sutherland and was pleased to find that Jim had ordered me another pint.

'Do you know what that bloke had in his garage?' I then began to list the treasures. Strangely, he did not appear to be very impressed. I then discovered why.

'I found a horse in one of mine this morning, and on Peter's beat there was a bloody blacksmith's!'

'All shown as empty, I suppose?'

He nodded.

It was the end of the third week when the last of the searchers ran finally out of enthusiasm. The whole scheme was saved from total humiliation by our sheer incompetence and by the public goodwill. The latter was best typified by the man from one of our estates who, after having his garage searched five times by five different groups, finally discovered that a sixth group had cut off his lock. 'I didn't really mind, guv'nor. The one that they put in its place was a lot better than my old one. In fact I think it was worth more than my car!'

# Totters and Company

I had no sooner arrived at the Metropolitan Police Training School in 1952 than part of it closed for repairs. During these two weeks — my first in the force — I was billeted in Blackheath Road Section House. From there, our class was driven daily to the training school by coach. In most respects, I was extremely fortunate in my first introduction to section-house life. Most of the section houses of that period were mid-Victorian and allegedly the setting for many of Dickens's workhouse stories. Blackheath Road Section House was newly built and clearly one of the best within the whole of the metropolis.

During my stay there, it became my practice to go down to the canteen around eleven o'clock each night for a cup of tea. There were scores of single policemen residing in the building, most of whom had been 'out on division' for some time. Our class of recruits was therefore an absolute godsend to many of these men. Nightly they would regale us with tales of their experiences, some of which may even have been true. It was during one such tale that my first introduction to the uncertainties of 'totting' took place.

Totters are usually no more than 'rag-and-bone' merchants. They work mainly from a horse and cart, and their base is usually a small yard. Television's *Steptoe* series captured them to perfection. While few totters are master-criminals, they are certainly not averse to a little 'opportunism'. One may therefore occasionally see an old horse standing forlornly within the precincts of a police station yard. There he will wait patiently for his owner to be bailed. By and large, policemen will have little to do with this animal. It is not that they do not love their lesser creatures, or that they are indifferent to their sufferings. It is simply that totters' horses are unfailingly cussed. It is a requirement of the breed. They also have such an inbred resentment of a police uniform that they make Ned Kelly look like our last commissioner.

Under the guidance of the most inarticulate totter, these animals daily negotiate the worst of London's rush-hour traffic without even a blink. But let a uniformed policeman attempt merely to lead them into a station yard and they will show all the smooth elegance of a skate-boarding rhino. A totter's horse is a pure anarchist. It knows of no law but its own. It does not attempt to inflict its views on others, it simply ignores them.

An experienced 'old sweat' with all of six months' service sat nonchalantly in the canteen and told me how he had captured a villainous totter that very afternoon. Suddenly the door swung open and an enormous police sergeant filled the whole doorway.

'Ah, Edwards, there you are! You nicked a totter this afternoon, yes?'

'Yes, sergeant,' agreed Edwards.

'Well, he was wanted on three previous counts of failing to answer bail. Therefore he will not be going anywhere until he goes to prison. As a result of your handiwork, we are now stuck with his bloody horse. How would you like to earn some overtime?'

'Well, yes, sarge, but how?'

'We have no facilities to keep a horse here. It will therefore

156

have to go to the animal pound at Woolwich. If you would care to walk it there, we could doubtless arrange for you to have a lift back. It should take you about – ' he studied his watch for some seconds, 'let me think – five miles there, five miles back – shall we say four hours?'

'Well, yeh, sarge, but what've I got to do?' asked the young man a little uncertainly.

'It's got a halter, all that you've got to do is to stand in front of the bloody thing and lead it. It's a straight road. Up the hill, across Blackheath and just keep going until you get there. An absolute piece of cake! Easiest four hours you'll ever earn!'

I had no more than eight days' service in the force, all spent in a classroom. I did, however, have great difficulty in restraining myself from uttering, 'Don't go, it stinks!'

'Do I have to wear my uniform, sarge?'

'Of course not, son,' said the sergeant. 'Not if you don't want to. You just wrap up warm-like and off you go. See me when you come back an' I'll see that you're all right for overtime.' He slyly winked his right eye at Edwards. 'Understand?'

'Yeh, okay, sarge.'

I decided to go into the yard to witness the departure of the pair. This yard was quite large and often used as a convenient overflow for the old police station some few streets away. I was surprised to see how the fog had rolled swiftly in from the river. Visibility was down to twelve yards and fading fast. I wouldn't have taken that creature to Woolwich for a month's wages, least of all for four hours' overtime.

The sergeant disappeared into the fog, while Edwards struggled into a variety of bulky clothing: boots, gloves, a couple of scarves, woollies and jumpers, all slipped over or on to the young policeman. Somewhere out in the gloom, we

157

could hear the muted, reassuring voice of the sergeant: 'Wow-boy!' 'There's a good boy.' 'C'mon boy!' Then a dramatic change of tone and direction: 'Give over, you lazy git!' Suddenly there was the sound of metal-tipped hooves on cobbles. A smiling and somewhat relieved-looking sergeant appeared out of the mist. He led an inoffensive piebald horse right up to the foot of the section-house steps.

'Here y'are, lad,' he said, cheerily handing over the rope lead. 'Just keep to the nearside of the road and you'll be fine.'

'Shouldn't I have a light or something, sarge?'

'No, there'll be nothing on the road except you. You'll do fine as you are. You mark my words, it'll be an absolute piece of cake!'

Gingerly, Edwards took the lead and, calling 'C'mon boy!' in a falsely confident voice, strode courageously off towards the fog. The horse remained stationary. The sergeant's mask then slipped a little as he gritted his teeth and smacked the creature loudly on the rump. 'Go'wun, you bastard, git moving!' The bastard did not move. Not as much as an eyelid.

'C'mon,' snapped the sergeant to me. 'We'll push!'

I was beginning to wish that I had never come out. The fog was now freezing fast and it had already penetrated my clothing. 'Well, sergeant,' I began.

'Don't just bloody stand there, push!'

We pushed, we pulled, we swore, we rested. It was while we rested that the horse moved slowly off into the fog.

'You've got him, lad, great!' yelled the sergeant excitedly. 'Off you go. And give us a ring when you get there!'

'I wouldn't do that job for a fortune, sarge,' I ventured quite daringly, as the sounds of the hooves faded slowly into the gloom.

'Neither would anyone else,' he confessed. 'But he's as silly

158

as a sackload of arse-holes. He'll do anything for four hours' overtime!'

I left the sergeant at the doorway. He stood peering out into the advancing perimeter of fog that was now barely nine yards away. I returned to the canteen and discovered that a soft brown crust had formed over my cup of tea. In order to thaw out, I propped myself against the radiator and ordered another tea. The cold damp air had temporarily driven away the advancing sleep from my body.

A section-house canteen rarely sleeps. Always there are comings and goings. Two men were in earnest conversation across the room, while on a table close by, three players sat studying their cards.

'D'you fancy making up a foursome?' the younger one offered.

I was either being highly honoured or they had been desperate for a fourth. I suspected the latter. 'If we can play on the table nearest to the radiator, yes!'

'Right,' nodded the speaker. 'Get yourself a chair.'

For some reason, I always assume in such situations that the other card-players will be better than myself. They were not. After two or three hands I began to make money. After forty minutes I was a pound up. A pound! One-sixth of my entire week's wages! Of course, there was no actual money lying on the table. One player was deputed to keep score, and any settling up that was required would be performed at the end of the game. Money on the table was very much frowned upon in police canteens. It was also illegal.

It is strange how thoughts of sleep can vanish from your mind when you are winning at cards. It was a quarter to one and I was wide awake when suddenly the sound of running footsteps could be heard pounding down the corridor. The canteen door burst open for the second time that night. A dishevelled and exhausted PC Edwards almost fell into the room.

'He's gone, I've lost 'im!' he gasped, fighting for breath. His face was red with the cold and his eyes were black from the fog. He looked like an escapee from some remote Siberian prison-camp.

'How did you manage to lose him, for Chrissake? I thought you had him on a lead,' said the older of my new companions.

'Er well, I did, but when I got to Blackheath – ' he paused for several seconds for breath. 'When I got to Blackheath, I decided to ride him.'

'And did you?'

'Well, no. Just as soon as I let go of the lead to get on – ' again a long pause, 'he buggered off!'

'Why couldn't you catch him?' I asked, unhelpfully.

'The fog's so thick up on that heath that you can't see the ground. I got lost twice coming down the hill.' He made six or seven great pants and then continued, 'Give us a hand to catch him, will you?'

'Look,' said the first speaker, 'go and see the sergeant. He's in the temporary hut across the yard. Tell him the whole story – well, perhaps not the *whole* story – and he'll organize something for you. Probably an official search-party, or something like that. When you've done that, come back here and we'll give you a hand to find the horse, okay?'

'Okay, thanks,' echoed Edwards gratefully. 'Christ, but it's cold out there,' he added as he turned and ran down the corridor.

The canteen door had barely closed when my three companions rocketed back their chairs with a unison that would have done credit to a formation dance-team. Not only did their chairs move together but so did their combined six legs.

It was very impressive. They were almost out of the room before I had time to look around.

'Whassamatter – what's up?' I cried, in a state of early panic.

One of the three paused for a second at the door. 'Unless you want to spend the rest of the night searching Blackheath for a horse, fuck off!'

I had caught them up before they had reached the end of the corridor. At the second flight of stairs I had passed them. I had experienced that fog once tonight, I didn't want a second dose. In something less than two minutes, I had reached the fourth floor, peeled off my clothes, leapt into bed and simulated sleep. Should anyone enter my room, I had hypothermia, comatosis, or perhaps even death. What I did not have was a desire to clump over fog-covered, frost-bound Blackheath. I considered myself an animal-lover up to a definite degree. This degree did not allow me to be posthumous. A sudden thought caused me to sit bolt upright. A pound! I had been winning a pound! But where was the slip of paper? Could I dare risk returning to the canteen to find it? The mad moment instantly passed. I knew I would not have returned to that canteen if I had been winning twenty pounds. Well, all right, perhaps for *twenty* pounds, but certainly not for anything under a fiver!

All training-school recruits had to assemble each morning in the canteen at eight o'clock. I had asked several people about the previous night's adventures but at first no one appeared to know anything about them. Just as we were lining up to board the coach, however, a section-house resident approached me.

'Were you the bloke asking about Ben Edwards and the totter's horse?'

'Yes, what happened to him?'

'Half-a-dozen of us spent four hours searching for it on the heath, meanwhile the bloody thing walked down here by itself.'

'How's Ben?'

'Gone to bed for a month's sulk, I should think. The sergeant refused him his overtime, because he lost the horse. Ben is not a happy man this morning.'

I never saw Ben again, but I certainly saw the horse. It became quite apparent that the animal had been sent on this earth to be the bane of all policemen. This function it carried out to perfection.

Some four months later, I had left the training school and been posted to Wharf Road Police Station. It was there, during my first period of early turn duty, that I next saw him. I was returning to the station to book off-duty when I noticed him pulling a cart laden with scrap-iron. It was a horse one could never forget. The head drooped very low as it nodded its way along the Walworth Road. I must confess that other than a quick recollection of that foggy night, nothing else registered in my mind. It was, after all, the last few minutes of my early turn shift and I had been awake since a quarter to five that morning.

Thoughts of a lovely two-hour sleep dominated my mind, as I turned into the back gate of the station. I was so tired that I practically collided with PC Reggie Dunn who was already on his way home. Commuting was not yet in fashion and several Wharf Road coppers lived on the manor, myself included. Reggie lived so close, barely five minutes' walk away, that he to'd and fro'd in uniform. Now if the main preoccupation of my mind was sleep, Reggie's would have been food. Reg enjoys his food more than anyone I have met. He wasn't a big man and he certainly wasn't fat but how he could eat! He not only had the proverbial hollow legs, but also hollow arms, ears and feet. If he could have been packed and dehydrated, he would have kept a commando unit going for a month. Occasionally his wife would place him on a diet. This was always doomed to failure. Reg considered that a diet was something that one ate between meals. When Reg is on his way home for dinner, one does not stand in his way. I did a swift side-step and gave a brief verbal acknowledgement. I doubt if he even noticed.

There then began a three-hour period which was among the blackest in Reggie's life, one that even now, after thirty years, saddens him to remember.

He was on it before he realized. There was a crowd, of course, there always is for an accident. There were angry words — these, too, can be anticipated. There was the expected damaged vehicle, all very predictable. What was totally unique, however, was the cause of the disturbance. Parked innocently alongside the kerb was a small Standard Eight saloon motor-car. Standing with one hind leg affixed neatly between the car bonnet and the bumper was a very angry horse!

Reg's first impression was one of horror. As far as he is concerned, any delay on his way home to dinner could be terminal. On the other hand, he was now *off* duty. Every policeman knows that the time taken to report an incident in such circumstances is one quarter of the time taken when he is actually *on* duty. (That is, providing he is not on official overtime, then it reverses.) In such circumstances, I have seen bus collisions and nine-pump fires reported in ten minutes flat. Anyone who was aware how much Reggie enjoyed his food would have bet that he would deal with this lot in five minutes.

Horses, however, have their own pace. Particularly this one. In addition, any horse that has his hoof firmly wedged in a motor-car is just not susceptible to persuasion. A passer-by who thought that he might be was carried away in an ambulance. A fireman who attempted to cut through the bumper-bar joined him. Meanwhile, the front of the car slowly disintegrated as the horse methodically, almost clinically, demolished it. After an hour, he had removed the headlamps, front wings, radiator, fan and most of the engine. He then turned with some relish to the transmission.

Five fire-engines, two ambulances and, three hours later, Reg, with the assistance of a vet, half the population of Walworth and the entire personnel of the Old Kent Road fire station released the horse from the perils of the internal combustion engine (or vice versa). The last vehicle to leave the scene was an ambulance. The driver had delayed because he suspected that Reg was suffering from an advanced stage of malnutrition. I suppose, in retrospect, the horse could be considered fortunate. After all, Reg could have eaten it. I daresay that thought crossed his mind. Whether that was the final straw for the animal I can only surmise, because I never saw him again. Perhaps he avoided the force after that, although it would be rather nice to think that he finished his days as horsemeat for police dogs.

Cussedness, however, is not purely a prerogative of totters' horses. Totters themselves are renowned for it. Perhaps it rubs off, or is even hereditary. I have long suspected that totters descend from their horses; after all, they frequently look alike and their temperaments can be identical. Take, for example, what happened to Chris Moore, a colleague of mine. One day, while patrolling in the area car, Chris spotted a totter's cart travelling in the opposite direction.

'We've just got to have a word with him!' exclaimed Chris. 'That load's a dead cert to have been nicked.' As soon as

Chris's companion turned his head, he could also see why. Swinging the car around, they overtook the cart and stopped a few yards in front of it.

'Morning, mate,' called Chris, cheerfully. 'What's on the cart, then?'

'Old iron, ennit? Anyone can see that. Is it an offence to collect old iron nowadays?'

'Yeh, but what's *underneath* the old iron?' asked Chris. 'That's what's interesting us.'

'Nuffink! Nuffink's underneath it. It's my game, ennit, collecting old iron. Whadda I want anyfing else for?'

'Well, let's just have a look, shall we?' said Chris's companion.

Both officers stood at the side of the cart and thrust their hands through the pieces of old scrap-metal that formed the bulk of the load.

'What's this, then?' asked Chris, pointing to the floor of the cart.

'Just a bit o' lining for the bottom o' me cart. I'm entitled to put down a bit o' lining for me own cart, ain't I?'

'Your "lining" looks suspiciously like new Wilton carpet to me,' said the second policeman.

New Wilton it was. Three rolls of it, to be precise.

The totter made no reply for a few moments, then he snapped angrily, 'All right, who wuz it? Who grassed me up? I bet it was – '

'No one grassed you up,' interrupted Chris. 'You did it yourself. You're the only totter that we've ever seen that covers rusty old scrap-iron with a new tarpaulin to keep out the rain! Did you nick that as well?'

They could tell by his face that he did.

To take the prisoner together with his horse and cart into the local police station entailed a two-mile drive.

'Tell you what,' said the driver to Chris. 'Get him to drive his cart into the nick and I'll follow behind. Perhaps you'd better ride with him, just in case he does anything silly.'

Chris agreed but the totter just folded his arms. 'You nicked me,' he announced. '*You* take it into the nick. I'm not going to.'

Secretly, Chris had been hoping that the totter would take just this stance. He had always fancied himself with a horse and cart. Now was his chance to try it. Chris climbed eagerly on to the front of the cart, as the totter climbed reluctantly into the back of the police car.

'Are you sure you can manage?' called out the driver anxiously. 'I don't want to hang about unnecessarily with a prisoner in the car. If I drive on, will I see you in the nick in a few minutes?'

'Sure!' called back Chris, confidently. 'I'll manage fine. Gidde up there!' He shook the reins and the horse slowly began to move forward.

The first thing that impressed itself on the new rider was the speed of the animal. It seemed barely to move. At this rate, thought Chris, it will take ages to get there. He tried shaking the reins again and called out a variety of 'c'mons' and 'gidde-ups', all to no avail. Resigning himself to a long plod, he settled back on to the sack-padded seat and decided to enjoy the ride.

The route to the police station was a straight journey along a main road, with just one right turn at a busy junction. As the pair approached this junction, Chris racked his brains for the necessary right-turn signal for the driver of a horse and cart. Suddenly the picture from an old highway code flashed into his mind – the whip! Of course, the whip had to be held straight out at right-angles, for all road-users to see. With ten yards to go to the stop-line, with Chris in full uniform and his right arm extended, the traffic lights changed to red against them.

'Whoa, boy!' he called as he tugged confidently on the reins.

But 'boy' did not 'whoa', nor did he make a right turn. Felix-like, he kept on walking, straight out into a four-laned highway packed with buses, motor-cars and lorries. The reaction of most of these drivers was really quite interesting. Here, they had a green-light right-of-way on a busy intersection. There, was a slowly lumbering totter's cart driven by a red-faced copper in uniform. This cart was not threading its way through the traffic so much as totally ignoring it. Bus drivers leaned swearing from their cabs, cyclists fell from their bikes and babies hid in their prams, but still the cart rolled on. Chris felt like a fifth horseman of the Apocalypse. War, pestilence and now . . .?

Somehow, and to his great astonishment, they cleared the junction unscathed, which was more than could be said for several other road-users. The truth of the situation finally struck the policeman some quarter of a mile past the junction. This horse was not going to deviate from a straight path, nor was he going to stop. It was like trying to control a runaway steam-roller. There was at least one hope of salvation. Two and a half miles straight ahead lay South Norwood Police Station. By an amazing stroke of good fortune, no traffic lights lay between them. There was unfortunately an enormous hill and numerous intersections but, having survived the last junction, Chris thought they could now manage anything.

With a great deal of lip-biting and even more luck, the cart rolled down the last few yards into South Norwood. Chris leapt from the seat and took hold of the halter. The horse turned like a lamb and obediently plodded into the small yard

167

at the rear of the station. The only problem now was that the prisoner was at Streatham and the evidence, to say nothing of the horse and the arresting officer, was the other side of the borough at South Norwood.

The laws of evidence unfortunately make no provision for totters' horses. Be that as it may, thought Chris, if the station officer wants them all at Streatham, then he can collect them his bloody self. This turned out to be less trouble than was at first feared. Station officers are usually placid creatures. They do occasionally have periods when they scream and throw things but on the whole they cope. They have to in order to survive. After all, if he is dealing with a complaint about a noisy police dog, a double accident in the station yard, an allegation by one prisoner of buggery by another, to say nothing of a flooding from a cell-toilet overflow, well, what's a totter's horse and cart at the wrong nick worth? Not much more than a very small ulcer.


No mention of London's totters would be complete without gypsies. Since local councils were compelled by central government to provide these travellers with permanent sites, they have been a varying problem. They tend to settle in an area for just a year or so, then move on. This can be unfortunate because it frequently takes that long for local people to adjust to their presence. Then, when everyone is quite used to them, there they are, gone!

While they are in the area, they do casual work, mainly consisting of totting. The only official camp-site that we had on the Wharf Road manor was little or no trouble. Nor did we experience any 'overflow problem' from the two large sites on neighbouring manors. In fact the main problem was hardly ever with the gypsies themselves, it was usually with their bloody horses. Although most of the travellers nowadays move around in rather sumptuous trailers, there are still a few who use the horse. I am therefore constantly amazed how a group of people who are so totally dependent on these animals for mobility allow the things to escape so often.

One dirty-white horse roamed Camberwell in the early hours of each morning for a whole week, defying all police attempts to catch it. It would suddenly appear out of the darkness like a ghostly apparition. Then, having scared the wits out of some half-asleep copper, disappear as quickly and silently as it arrived. Many's the policeman who had his fantasy of scoring the winning goal at Wembley, or of ravishing Sophia Loren, dashed by this equine phantom.

John Robertson, a young, slim Scot from Glasgow, had been posted to the Camberwell end of our manor for the last five nights. He had seen the horse on three separate occasions but had been unable to get anywhere near it. He had wondered where it went to during daylight hours. Probably it returned through the granite walls of the Tower of London. It was while he was taking a penalty for Celtic in the last minute of the European Cup Final that he turned into Camberwell Grove. Sixty yards ahead of him and clearly illuminated under the street light was the ghost horse. It stood quietly on the pavement, munching away at some morsel it had found in a garden hedge.

John reached instinctively for his bat-phone. He realized there was no way that he could capture the thing by himself, it was far too wary. His personal radio was of the old type which had its aerial secreted away in a wide canvas strap that ran diagonally across his body. This type was in the process of being replaced. John's particular radio offered the best reason as to why this change was considered necessary. It didn't work.

He made a couple of half-hearted attempts to communicate with the station but received nothing except a few phuts and splutters in reply. Summoning up all of his Celtic courage, he approached the nibbling animal. To his surprise, the creature did not seem unduly concerned. At that moment, 'c'mon, boy' was about the only horse command that John could lay his tongue to. He was not even sure what it meant. He was also fairly certain that the horse wouldn't either. Any horse that was accustomed to following Romany instructions was not going to leap into obedience by a single command in thick Glaswegian. Sure enough, his 'c'mon, boy' received the scant attention it deserved and the animal continued to chew the hedge.

John then wondered if perhaps he could try to lead the thing down to Camberwell Police Station. There he could use the telephone and rally some sort of assistance. He placed his hand under the horse's neck and began to pull the head around. To his surprise, after some initial token resistance the horse responded. John gave another 'c'mon, boy' for good measure and the pair of them began to stroll casually down the hill.

Having travelled some forty yards, whatever mechanism triggers obstinacy in a horse's brain suddenly clicked into operation. The animal stopped dead. All the pulling, tugging and old Celtic oaths made not the slightest difference. After a couple of minutes of this confrontation, the horse realized that the nearby hedge was just as intriguing as the one he had recently vacated. Nudging John aside, he walked across the pavement and immediately began to rummage.

John suddenly had a brainwave. He unclipped his batphone from his strap and slipped it into his back pocket. He looped the strap over the horse's head and hooked the end to a thick branch in the hedge. If he could manage to keep the horse in this one spot, then he could run down to Camberwell for assistance. The horse seemed quite happy to let the young policeman play and offered no resistance, although the strap most certainly restricted his movements.

Some minutes later, John burst into the police office. There he blurted out to the astonished sole occupier, WPC Freda Cookson, his valiant struggle with the horse.

'Ye ring fer assistance, lassie, I'll be going back ter yon creature.'

'Lassie' was just about to do John's bidding when the first customer for hours came into the station office. He was a delivery driver for a wholesale newsagent and his diesel van throbbed smokily outside.

' 'Ere, mate!' he said to the departing John, 'I've just seen an 'orse tied up in Camberwell Grove. Fair cruel it was. It only 'ad a little strap ararnd 'is neck. The poor fing could 'ardly git his breff.'

'Aye, it's alreet,' called back John, curtly, 'it's being dealt with. Everything is under control.'

'Oh!' said the man, now showing some concern. 'I 'ope I did right, then, 'cos I undone the strap.'

'Ye what!!'

'I, er, I undid the strap,' repeated the man, now backing away.

'Where's the horse now?'

'Er, well, 'e's legged it orf up the 'ill. I'm sorry, did I do wrong, then?'

'If I was you I'd leave,' whispered Freda confidentially to the driver.

'Yeh, yeh. I fink I will.' He disappeared within seconds in a great puff of blue cancerous smoke.

There was no further sign of the horse for some weeks. Then, I am proud to say, I bravely assisted in its capture.

This was accomplished in a most unusual manner – at one in the morning with a pint in my hand.

Willie Williams was an old-fashioned publican. He ran his pub firmly and well. He had been a friend for many years and, on his retirement, gave a private party in his saloon bar behind closed doors. The guests were all his regulars, of whom was included myself and two other colleagues from Wharf Road Police Station. Because of the position where I sat in the bar, I acquired the task of locking the door firmly as each guest left. I was just about to close the door on a departing group when a dramatic screech of tyres caused me to look outside into the street. A police car had braked to a halt on the far side of the road and the two occupants had leapt hastily out.

Now I have always noticed how, whenever I sit drinking in a pub, it becomes much easier to theorize about every aspect of crime. It just seems that I have this flair to become wise and perceptive in a public-house atmosphere. Having been a recipient of three hours of Willie's hospitality, I was undoubtedly wiser and more perceptive than I had been for some years. I just knew that if I rushed out to offer my off-duty assistance, everyone concerned would find my perception a great asset. I had followed my two fellow-officers some distance into a newly completed housing estate before I discovered that I was still holding my pint jug in my hand.

The estate was a beautiful new low-rise complex. Much of the corrugated fencing was still around it and only a sprinkling of families had yet taken up residence. Houses like these are particularly vulnerable at such times, with fixtures and fittings being most prized.

I caught up with the two officers when they paused at a corner. There they tilted their heads to one side in a futile attempt to increase their audible powers.

'Wassa-marra, lads?' I asked.

'Shsssssss!' hissed Freda Cookson, obviously not too thrilled with either my voice or my eyesight.

'What's up, then?' I stage-whispered.

'Will-you-be-quiet! Lynda has sent a call up on her bat-phone but her radio's a bit useless and we think that she is here somewhere. Now just be quiet and listen!'

'LYN-DA!' I chorused. 'Where a-r-e you?'

I was saved from the wrath of my colleagues by an answering cry.

'Here! I'm here!'

Freda paused before tearing my throat out and they both ran to the next corner. I followed gamely behind. As I turned the corner, I could see the reason for Lynda's garbled message. She stood in a small entrance that led alongside one of the new bungalows. Standing in front of her and completely blocking her exit was our phantom white horse!

The animal did not appear intimidating in any way whatever. He simply seemed to find great satisfaction in standing and staring at the girl. I suddenly felt a great affinity with him. I had experienced the same feelings myself about Lynda on a number of occasions.

On seeing us he turned and nodded his head vigorously up and down several times. He then began to trot towards us. Freda and the driver sensibly disappeared into a side alley. I was made of sterner stuff. After three hours in Willie's pub, I was not only perceptive about crime-fighting but I was more than a little useful at steer-wrestling. Being left-handed, I transferred my pint to my right hand in order to give my best to the approaching combat. As he came nearer, the animal's approach slowed appreciably. When he was barely three feet away, he stopped dead. Freda Cookson said afterwards that she had not been at all surprised by this. A pint-laden,

173

one-armed, drunken steer-wrestler was a puzzling sight even for a phantom horse, she claimed.

I proved by my next remark that I was magnanimous enough to mediate. 'Whoa, boy. There's a good horse!'

I put my lethal left arm forward to offer a conciliatory but firm pat. The horse, however, was now showing a great deal of interest in my right arm, or, at least, in the pint – or what was left of it after spillages and odd sips – that was on the end of it. I gallantly tipped the glass forward so the beer reached the rim of the glass. With surprising ease, my new friend managed to finish the contents with a minimum amount of loss. I then patted that horse with a fondness that is found only among drinking pals.

'I s'pose it's his round now, is it?' said Freda, acidly.

The police van had now arrived and the tow-rope was looped around the horse's neck. Because of his unrequited love for the fair Lynda, she was nominated to walk him into the station. It was suggested that she walk beside him and not directly in front of him. Horses can, after all, do such peculiar things, especially when they've been drinking.

Declining the offer to be thrown into the back of the police van, I bid everyone, including the horse, a loving farewell. I returned to The Feathers with an empty glass and a heart-warming story for Willie. Sadly, he received neither. My absence had been taken as desertion and I was now locked out.

I suddenly thought how typical that was of a policeman's life. I risk my life and limb and what have I got to show for it? Shut out of a pub with an empty glass.

# A Special Lady

The Special Constabulary dates back in one form or another to the time of Charles the Second. This constabulary was resurrected by various governments in times of crisis over the next three hundred years: in the 1840s the early Victorians used special constables to combat the threat from the Chartists; the Edwardians likewise used them during the industrial unrest in the early part of this century. Finally at the beginning of the 1914–18 war the Special Constabulary was organized into a body similar to the present-day one: a voluntary, part-time organization, paid only their expenses. Their prime function in 1914 was to prevent German infiltrators from interfering with the nation's water supply. The country's water supply was in greater danger of pollution from little boys piddling on river banks than ever it was from the dreaded hun, but the fact that no one appeared to have died from drinking the stuff seemed to justify the formation of the Special Constabulary.

Since that rather eccentric origin, they have risen to many occasions, playing significant parts in, for example, the general strike of 1926 and the 1939–45 war. They remain, however, misunderstood people within the force. Although today they are more accepted than they were even twenty years ago, some resentment towards them is still felt, for a variety of reasons. For instance, the time spent on training a special is probably one-hundredth of that spent on their full-time counterparts. Secondly, should a serving policeman fail his probationary exam, he can be dismissed from the force, and many are. He could by that time have received thousands of hours of instruction and have served almost two years on the streets. Yet a special constable receives up to two hours a week training over twenty-three weeks, supplemented by another thirty-two hours on the streets. A minimum of seventy-eight hours. Yet the special can then walk the same streets as the serving policeman, turn the same corners and be expected to cope with the same reaction, hostile or welcoming. It is probably for this reason more than any other that the resentment arises.

My first experience of this in-built annoyance came soon after I joined the force. A driver from the local bus-garage was working as a special constable at Wharf Road. 'Can you imagine what would happen,' said an old-time copper to me, 'if I went down to his garage on my day off and drove his bus? They'd be out on strike afore yer could blink. That's why I don't like 'em. There's no place for 'em here!' Well, I did not see the equation then and I don't see it now. It was considered by the rank and file of the force that the Special Constabulary somehow deprived us of our birthright. Once I got around to giving the matter some thought, I could not see how they made one ha'penny worth of difference to our conditions, one way or another. In fact the biggest problem with the specials is not the reluctance of the lower ranks to accept them as much as the inability of the hierarchy to know what the hell to do with them. They are used gleefully for ceremonial occasions, such as Trooping the Colour, Beating the Retreat, royal processions and state visits, but after that the problems arise.

Many police stations, for example, have a regular police inspector who has a direct responsibility for specials who are posted to his station. If this inspector has just one or two specials to worry about, then he can get by. It is when he suddenly finds himself with several that his troubles really begin. How on earth does he keep them occupied? A day's attachment in the front office, another on the area car. Even a few hours in a police-boat if the river is near enough, but after that? Ideally, an experienced special constable would help in the training of another, but frequently, like their full-time colleagues, they do not stay long enough to become experienced.

Occasionally a whole flurry of specials will arrive at a station at around the same time. When that happens, the liaison officer spreads them around like circulars. One only has to stop to pass the time of day for him to say: 'Oh! Have you had a special lately?' Even ignoring the whole field of sexual connotation in that little query, it is no wonder that other policemen begin to avoid him. Eventually, in a fit of total desperation, he will try to devise a scheme or rota system for the deployment of these ladies and gentlemen. We had one such scheme at Wharf Road.

'Harry,' said Inspector Wood in an unusually affable manner. 'I have seven special constables to deploy. How about taking one around your patch on a regular basis?'

'Not keen, guv,' I responded. Experience had taught me never to give a definite answer to any supervising officer. One always needs room to manoeuvre.

'Well, you may soon have no choice,' he replied, his new-found affability already slipping. 'With seven of them here, it's a full-time job just knowing what to do with them. If I don't get some volunteers soon, then it's going to become compulsory. So make your choice!'

'I tell you what,' I answered, realizing that if I entered the debate before the rest of my colleagues I could at least have a say in exactly who I was allocated, 'I'll take out any special constable for four hours each week, on one condition.'

His eyes narrowed and at first he said nothing. Then, shaking his head in disgust at his own curiosity, he snapped suspiciously, 'Well, what is it?'

'It's got to be one of the girls. I don't care which one it is but it must be one of the three young ladies.'

'Oh yeh? Why the girls, then? I won't think you're a pouff if you take out a fellah, you know. The girls are, well – ' He paused with only slight embarrassment. 'Well, they're a bit young for you, aren't they?'

'Well, I don't actually plan to elope with any of them. It's just that – ' I paused, trying to pick my words carefully. 'Well, a couple of those blokes look a bit "suspect" to me. Whereas all three girls seem like nice kids. Therefore, as I am not in the business of missionary work, I'd sooner take out a "nice-kid" girl, than a "suspect" bloke.'

The strange aspect of that exchange was that he never once queried my 'suspect' claim. Yet it was in this casual conversation that the whole problem of some special constables was indirectly touched upon. Namely, why do they join? Nine times out of ten, a special constable joins for one of two reasons. First, he or she wishes to be of some service to the community – great! Secondly, he or she, being quite happy in their present employment, wishes to feel the water of the force before committing themselves full-time. Equally laudable and eminently sensible. There is, however, a third and quite sinister reason why a very small percentage of people become specials. This is the uniform syndrome. They join because for a couple of hours each week they can parade around the streets in uniform with a considerable amount of power. This novelty does wear off very quickly and they soon leave the service or are dismissed. Nevertheless, I had strong suspicions about two of our male specials.

'Okay, you're on. You are allocated – let me see – ' Wood paused and looked down his list. 'Yes, you're allocated Julia Barratt. Like you say, she's a nice kid, so look after her, eh?'

I walked thoughtfully away from the inspector. I felt that I was already a goal up on my colleagues. One thing was sure, whoever was allocated either of the two weirdos would be furious. That cheered me immensely!

My first patrol with Miss Barratt was scheduled for the following Wednesday afternoon between 2 and 6 pm. I was already beginning to worry. I had just agreed to spend four hours a week with this young lady, probably for the next six months at least. It could well be likened to hospital-visiting. Supposing we didn't get on? I had, of course, seen her around the station, but other than the occasional 'Morning', we had not even spoken. Four hours can be an eternity if the chemistry is wrong. And this was a self-inflicted wound!

I quickly re-scheduled a visit to a local secondary school to that Wednesday afternoon. An hour spent in the classrooms would take up at least one quarter of my stint with the special constable. A twenty-minute walk either way would take up even more time. Yet was this, I wondered, the best approach I could make? It did seem a little negative, to say the least.

On Wednesday it rained. During the next eighteen months, I must have spent hundreds of hours and walked scores of miles in that young lady's company; on most of them it poured. There were more wet Wednesdays in Walworth between 1974 and early 1976 than in the whole of the South American rain-forests. Julia Barratt was incredible. She only had to put on her uniform for entire anti-cyclones to dissolve. At one o'clock over the whole of Great Britain there would be nothing but a slight mist over Rockall. By two o'clock, south-east London would be awash. When she ceased her

Wednesday afternoon patrols with me, the country then had its driest summer since records were kept.

As we bowed our heads and walked into the storm towards the school, I decided to use the time to become better acquainted with the girl. She told me that she worked as a civilian at Scotland Yard. She had serious thoughts about joining the Metropolitan Police and was using the Special Constabulary as a feeler. Julia was very much a local girl. Her knowledge of the Wharf Road manor was therefore infinitely greater than many of my professional colleagues. She was a good-looking girl in her early twenties, with a fine complexion and a ready smile. Oh yes, this was definitely one of my better ideas!

While threading our way through the puddles, I began to explain to her the purpose of these school visits. 'We're going into Newington Annexe school, where I'm due to give a talk to a couple of classes. You may find it of some interest. If when I'm talking you feel like joining in, then don't! This is *not* an easy school. I wouldn't be a teacher there for a fortune!'

We climbed the stairs to the headmaster's office but met him en route. I introduced him to Julia and began to speak to him about a recurring complaint from a nearby resident. This concerned several of the boys from the school who had taken to terrorizing a local household which consisted of middle-aged parents and an invalid son of about twenty. The son had been waiting some time for a kidney transplant. While he was waiting, he had to undergo three blood-changes each week on a dialysis machine. This function was carried out at home by himself and his parents. The result was that his bedroom had taken on the appearance of a rather well-equipped operating theatre. This life-saving but grim ritual did not stop stones from crashing at or through his windows. These missiles would frequently be hurled while he was actually lying on the machine. From the timing of these raids, there was no doubt where the boys came from – Newington Annexe school.

As we stood discussing this problem, the sound of running footsteps caught my attention. The school corridors were very narrow and Mr Richards, the headmaster, strictly enforced the 'no running' rule. A large sixteen-year-old West Indian youth came hurtling along the corridor. On seeing the headmaster, he skidded to a halt, though not before he collided with the headmaster.

'Look where you are going, Williams!' said the head sharply. 'You know very well that you are not supposed to run in the corridors!'

I suppose that I was expecting the usual schoolboy excuse, such as 'It wasn't me sir!' or 'I was pushed by another boy, sir!' or perhaps even 'Yardley told me to do it, sir!' What I was definitely not expecting, was the boy's actual response: 'Why? You shouldn't have been there, man. Why are you talking to the fuzz anyway?' With that, he chewed on some unseen gum and provocatively turned his back on the headmaster.

I looked instinctively across at Julia. I was reasonably fit at the time and my reactions were probably a little quicker than most – but I almost didn't make it. Her arm was drawn back to its maximum and was about to rocket forward. I quickly seized her arm. Even through her raincoat, I felt the muscles tightened powerfully. Now Julia was a lovely girl in very many ways but she would never be a delicate, fragile, consumptive heroine. She was in fact a very wholesome lass. Being the eldest of six children, her duties in bringing up the Barratt clan had doubtless included delivering the occasional wallop. Leroy Clement Williams was just about to get his. I immediately realized that one restraining hand was not going to be enough. I quickly dispatched the second to dissuade her. Her head turned sharply towards me and her eyes flashed out a primeval warning.

'No, Julia! No!' I cried, as I tried desperately to soothe her down. 'We do not belt school kids in front of their headmaster. *Particularly* not in front of their headmaster!'

'But didn't you see? Didn't you hear? My brothers would never have been allowed – '

'Julia! He's *not* your brother!'

'You're dead right he's not my brother! I would have killed him if he was, and so would my mum!'

'Williams!' called the headmaster, white with embarrassment. 'Come here at once!'

The boy turned on his heel. He swayed rhythmically and walked back to within a few feet of the headmaster. Insolence oozed from every pore.

'Don't worry 'bout it, man. Don't worry 'bout it at all.'

There was a restrained roar from deep inside the avenging Miss Barratt. Fortunately for the boy, he had already turned once again and was halfway down the staircase and on his way out of the building. Having lost Leroy, the young lady then turned her attention to me.

'What'd you stop me for?' she demanded.

'Because you were going to belt him, that's why!'

'I know I was! He deserved it, didn't he? Have you ever seen a kid who deserved it more? I just can't stand helplessly around listening to any kid talk to someone like that.'

'But he was in school!' I explained.

'So?'

'Look, if you belt a kid in his own school, in front of his own headmaster, you'd have Jonathan Dimbleby, the *Panorama* camera-team and the entire staff of the National Council for Civil Liberties down at the nick tomorrow! It was on school premises and it is the job of the headmaster.

It's not your fight, d'you understand?'

'He's quite right, Miss,' said the head gently. 'But thank you just the same.'

Turning his attention to me once again, the headmaster expressed his concern about the continuation of the vendetta against the kidney sufferer.

'How is he?' he asked anxiously. 'Do you think it would help if I went over and apologized?'

'Why don't you take some boys with you?' suggested Julia. 'It might be a good idea if they could see exactly what suffering they are causing.'

'How's he going to do that?' I scoffed. 'He's got over three hundred and fifty boys in this school. We don't even know which ones are causing the problem!'

'I wouldn't be too sure about that,' murmured the head. 'I bet I could narrow it down.'

'To what?' persisted Julia.

'Oh, I don't know, about thirty or so, I should think.'

'Well, can't we take them over a few at a time? It's only two minutes' walk away.'

The headmaster bit his lip thoughtfully. 'She could well have a point there, you know,' he said looking at me through half-closed eyes. 'Shall we go over and see? They can only say "no", after all.'

The rain had now eased and the sun peeped through as the three of us crossed the wet road towards the specially adapted, council-owned bungalow. Mr Randleston opened the door and was quite surprised to see the three of us. He nevertheless readily fell in with Julia's idea.

'There's not very much room in the bedroom, what with the equipment, but we could certainly squeeze in about four kids at a time.'

'When can we begin?' asked the head, eagerly.

183

'Well, how about now?' replied the overwhelmed Randleston. 'My son is at home and he could show them everything, including exactly how the machine works.'

We were all now quite fired with the idea. The plan was for the head to select the suitable candidates and for Julia and me to escort them over to the bungalow, four at a time.

'Here you are!' chirped the head, as he handed the first four boys over to me. 'You'll find it quite fascinating, lads, quite fascinating.'

I must say the 'lads' did not seem to share their headmaster's enthusiasm. There was a great deal of suspicion on those four faces. Within a couple of minutes, I had handed the four boys to Mr Randleston. I returned to the school in time to meet Julia with her group.

'Don't forget,' I whispered to her, 'you're not allowed to bash 'em!'

She narrowed her eyes threateningly and marched the quartet briskly away.

Within a few minutes, I had again reached the bungalow, this time with my second group. I was greeted by an amazing sight. The first group were sitting on the damp kerbstone, looking positively ashen. Three of them were being sick and the other one looked about to be. The door of the bungalow then burst open and Julia's four came tumbling out. Two of them instantly vomited into the road. I immediately stopped my four from entering. Eight kids had now gone into that place and within a few minutes, five of them were spewing their hearts up!

'What on earth's happening?' I demanded.

'He's fantastic!' she cried. 'He shows them just about everything. He shows them where the blood enters and leaves his body. He's shown them the needles, the pumps and even the blood-stain up the wall, where the tube came off last night!'

'Bloody hell! We can't take the kids in there if they are all going to be sick!'

'Of course we can! There's already eight kids there who'll never throw another stone through his windows!'

'Well, I'm not too sure about this,' I bleated, weakly. 'I'll have to have a word with Richards first.'

'Okay, while you're gone I'll take these new four in for you.' That seemed a very noble gesture to me. I did not relish the idea of joining that vomiting bunch on the pavement one little bit.

When I explained to the head what had happened, he was over the moon. 'That's fantastic! Do you think we could get the whole school over there? No, that's selfish, but I would like to take at least another two dozen!'

'You think that it's a good idea to continue, then?' I asked, uncertainly.

'Good idea? It's absolutely bloody marvellous! The girl's a genius!'

Julia and I seemed to go back and forth over that road dozens of times. I never discovered exactly how many boys we escorted but there were so many that I swear he sent some down twice. The boys' reactions in the end were due simply to mass hysteria. Some of them became sick just by crossing the road.

The long-term results, however, were incredible. Not only did the aggravation end but a relationship between the school and Randleston developed that lasted until the family moved away some two years later.

My first-day impressions of Special Constable Julia Barratt were, not surprisingly, impressive. During the next few months I became even more impressed. Her excellent, down-to-earth good sense, made itself felt in every street situation.

One afternoon some three months later, Julia and I found ourselves in a very familiar situation, in a deep doorway sheltering from the rain.

'I've been thinking of applying to join the police force on a full-time basis,' she said. 'What d'you think about that?'

'I've met few people who have been more suitable,' I answered with a candour that surprised even me. 'Ninety per cent of this job is commonsense. You could do it standing on your head. You are really cut out for it. Specially now that you've stopped bashing kids! If you'd like me to, I'll have a word with Inspector Wood. I assume you've told him?'

'Yes, I mentioned it to him a few days ago. He seemed quite keen. Incidentally, I'm being promoted to sergeant, so watch it!'

Some days later, I spoke to Wood but he had forestalled me. 'I know what you're going to say, and you're right. Just as soon as she applies officially, I'll make a covering report. I don't see any problems. Miss Barratt will, I believe, be a real asset to this force.'

Anyone applying to join the Metropolitan Police needs time, oodles of it for preference. No matter how strong the recruiting campaigns may be, they are never matched by the administration work. Some months therefore elapsed before Julia heard anything definite.

'They won't have me,' she said sadly, one damp Wednesday afternoon.

'Whyever not?' I asked, genuinely surprised.

'They say that I have defective vision in one eye.'

'Well, have you?'

'I s'pose that I must have. But it doesn't seem to prevent me being a "special", though, does it?' she answered ruefully. 'Anyway, I'm going to try some of the other police forces around London. P'raps they'd like a Nelson,' she added, already brightening up.

'Such as?'

'Kent, Essex and perhaps Surrey.'

'It rains there too, you know,' I pointed out.

She said little for the rest of the day and I could see that she was far more disappointed than she was prepared to admit.

After another couple of months, all her applications had been acknowledged. She had failed them all because of the defect in her vision. This confirmation from the other forces seemed somehow to redress the balance. She was now her old self again. Although she continued to patrol with me each Wednesday, she would also attend the station on other occasions throughout the week. Sometimes I thought she was there more than I was. In fact Sunday was the only day I never saw her around. Eventually we ceased our Wednesday afternoon patrols. She was now far too competent to need any supervising from me and was in fact supervising special constables herself.

I had not seen Julia for some weeks when, one bleak wet Sunday, I was hastily summoned to join most of the personnel at Wharf Road for a surprise National Front march. She was the first person I saw as I entered the station.

'Julia!' I called, as ever really pleased to see her. 'What are you doing here on a Sunday? I thought Sunday was your day for lying in bed.'

'Well, it is usually but they telephoned me and asked if I could help out.'

'Who telephoned you?'

'None other than the chief superintendent, would you believe! Apparently, because of the National Front march there is nobody left at the station to cover East Street market. He rang me and asked if I could come and look after it. I've rolled straight out of bed, does it show?'

'No, you look gorgeous, but what do you mean "look after" the market? You and who else?'

'Just me. I'm all that's on today.'

'But that's nonsense! It's an absolute contradiction! Why on earth did you agree to come in?'

'Well,' she began, quite bewildered at my brusque approach, 'it's just to help out. Like I told you, he said that he didn't have anybody else, so what could I do? I couldn't let him down. After all, I was only dozing in bed.'

'Couldn't let him down!' I snorted. 'Do you realize what's happened? They have told you that you are incapable of performing this job full-time because you have faulty vision, yes?'

'Er, yes, yes I suppose that they have,' she agreed, somewhat grudgingly.

'But now, because it suits them, your vision is quite satisfactory. Half an hour ago, as far as the police force was concerned, you were as blind as a premature mole. Now I suppose you can see like a hawk?'

'That's a bit sweeping!'

'No, it's not! Anything between ten and fifteen thousand people attend that market on a Sunday morning. Pick-pockets, purse-snatchers and fly-pitchers. The whole bloody area comes to a standstill for four hours. But you, you with your defective vision, you can go down there on your own and cover a market that would normally have a dozen coppers! They are taking a monumental liberty with you. They are using you simply as a bloody convenience!'

She looked stunned. 'I never thought of it like that.' She bit her lip for a second or two. She then looked up at me with moist eyes and said quietly, 'I'll do the market this morning because I promised that I would. But when I have finished,

I'm coming back to the station and I'm resigning.'

'But Julia, I didn't mean — '

It was too late. She did not appear even to have heard me. She adjusted her hat and walked out into the street. It had stopped raining.

## The Long New Year

I hate punctures. The tiniest piece of glass in my cycle tyre fills me with gloom and bad temper. It's not that I don't know how to mend them, I do. It's just that the instant I attempt any job which involves a spanner, serenity, compassion and good humour vanish. They are replaced by neurosis, truculence and blood-lust. Nothing can make such an instant reversal in one person's character as a spanner can on mine.

I don't really understand why I make such a big issue of punctures. I have seen international cycle races where the victim of a burst tyre has changed the whole lot, almost before his wheel has stopped turning. Yet I need to be left alone at such times. I will swear, talk to myself and throw things.

At the time of my interruption, I had actually mended the thing. I was, however, at the crucial stage of attempting to replace the cycle tyre on the wheel rim. This, as any cyclist will tell you, is where you realize that every tyre ever made is exactly half an inch shorter than its corresponding rim. To twist that tyre into place is like trying to give a horse a 'hot-wrist'. My teeth bit deep into my tongue, my eyes bulged and the skin parted painfully from my knuckles. Still the rotten thing would not budge.

'Ah, Constable Cole!'

I shut my eyes in silent prayer. No, not Peter Cage! Please don't let it be Peter Cage. Not at a time like this.

'Good morning, Constable Cole. I'm about to do you a favour.'

It was worse than I thought. It was not only him, but he was about to do me a favour! Tribulation on tribulation. I did a rapid mental calculation. What would I get for belting a sergeant? Reprimand? Fined two weeks' pay? Perhaps even dismissal? That would be worth it, I thought; I'm leaving the force soon anyway. Yes, I would definitely belt him. I slowly eased myself to my feet and my blood changed direction. It ceased pouring out of my gashed opened knuckles and reversed into my poor screwed-up limbs.

'Now, now, constable, don't be cross. How would you care to go to a nice New Year's Eve party? There's free food, doubtlessly free booze and, if you're lucky, free girls. Mind you,' he said, looking at me thoughtfully, 'in your case you *really* would have to be lucky.'

'Sergeant!' I said, threateningly. 'You should know better than to speak to me when I am mending a puncture. And before you go any further, I am not doing duty in Trafalgar Square on New Year's Eve!'

'Yes, you are,' he said coaxingly. 'You'll like it up there, it's nice. All of those young ladies queuing up to kiss the poor policemen. It'd be right up your street. Might even find a couple of old crones for you! It's the last chance that you're going to get, you know. After all, you're getting on now, all of that excitement hardens the arteries. Come on, give us a smile and I'll put your name forward for your last fling.' He made an exaggerated motion of wetting his pencil with his tongue and scrawling my number down on his clipboard. 'Six, oh, er, let me see.' He glanced studiously down to the third number on my shoulder. 'Ah, of course, four! That's it, 604. What a nice number that is.' With that, the tormenting bugger walked away. Of course he knew my number just as well as he knew his own but he was joyfully prolonging my misery. 'Parade at Wharf Road at 5.45 pm,' he called back over his shoulder.

'What time!' I let go of the last remaining two inches of tyre.

He stopped and turned. 'Five forty-five,' he repeated, very slowly and deliberately. 'Oh dear, you really are getting on, your hearing's going. Five forty-five is a quarter to six, understand?' He mouthed the last four words very slowly and deliberately. Shaking his head, he resumed his journey away from me.

I was due to start work six and a quarter hours before midnight and Trafalgar Square was only one and a half miles away! I really did have the miseries now. I had originally been scheduled to work nine-to-five on New Year's Eve. Oh well, it would make a change. I looked down at my tyre, I swear those two remaining inches had now grown. The whole bloody tyre was back off the rim.

New Year's Eve turned out to be a particularly mild day. Our briefing was a straightforward affair, given to us by Inspector Heckman from neighbouring Peckham Police Station. 'This is not a "them-v-us" situation. The crowds at these do's are ninety-nine-per-cent good-natured and are there purely to enjoy themselves. You'll get kissed to death but don't indulge too much in their liquid hospitality. I do not wish to have to fish inebriated coppers from the fountains. There will, of course, be the occasional pickpocket and purse-snatcher and we therefore have a large plain-clothes squad working in the square.'

'How will we know them?' asked a young constable from Peckham.

'Y . . . e . . . s,' sighed the inspector, 'I was hoping that you wouldn't ask that, because it's a little unbelievable. Apart from their warrant cards, which you'll usually be too far away to see, they'll be carrying what looks suspiciously like,' he paused again, 'a prostitute's vibrator.' He immediately put up his hands to forestall the rush of expected questions. 'Don't ask me why, I don't know myself, but if some total stranger advances on you and flashes what looks very much like a dildo, he's not a pervert but a detective and he doubtless needs your help. I think that's about it. Anyone got any questions?'

'Just one, sir,' said the young Peckham constable. 'What have the lady detectives been issued with, inflatable dolls?'

Heckman was not to be drawn, however, and two minutes later we filed out of the canteen and on to our coach.

A little after nine o'clock, the Wharf Road group took up a position on the east side of the square, immediately in front of South Africa House. We were posted in pairs and my partner was Dave Saunders, a community-cop colleague. Dave was a former guardsman about six feet three inches in height and sixteen stones in weight. My five feet nine and eleven and a half stone found that rather reassuring.

Hundreds of policemen were posted all around the square. There were nine or ten based beside each of the lions and dozens more on the base of Nelson's column. A whole fleet of ambulances stretched away down the Mall towards Buckingham Palace, and a large casualty-clearing station was positioned on the south side of the square. It looked like the preparation for a prearranged battle.

In front of South Africa House is a large basement area. It is about twelve feet wide and some twenty feet in depth. Filled with water and a shoal of piranha, it would make a terrific moat. Dave and I took up a position at the south end of the parapet that divides the area from the pavement. This was just about the least desired position in the whole vicinity, the reason being the nearby hamburger stall that was wedged in a recess.

Somehow hamburger stalls and hamburger sellers, particularly hamburger sellers, always look thoroughly unwholesome. In addition, I usually find the smells from both quite appalling. This stall was no exception. It was staffed by a grossly overweight, spotty young man of some eighteen years. He was as wide as he was tall and his sales line consisted solely of, 'Git yer 'amburgers 'ere! Greatest afro-dizy-acks in the world!' I assumed that someone had once told him the meaning of the word aphrodisiac and it had fired his imagination.

Oddly enough, I never once heard him call out the price. I surmised they were quite expensive, because after a brief conversation with an enquiring customer he turned to me and asked me the meaning of the word 'parasite'.

'How come you know aphrodisiac but don't know parasite?' I asked, genuinely curious.

'I fort parasite was an umbrella but I wanted to be sure,' he countered.

By nine-thirty, the square was filling up fast. The first of the New Year's Eve kisses were being dispatched. I was quite alarmed when an ancient, drunken old witch advanced on me amorously. I had all the apprehension of a frightened virgin. I kept thinking that she was a plant by Peter Cage. Dave and I were reprieved in the nick of time by Inspector Heckman. There had been a reshuffling of our position and we were therefore moved some twenty-five yards further south, to the corner of Trafalgar Square and the Strand.

It took us some minutes to negotiate that short distance and we were pleased to discover a shallow doorway at the location. This doorway was only recessed some eighteen inches but it provided some shelter from the milling and exhausting crowd. There were just two narrow steps that led up to a pair of huge iron doors, some ten feet in height. Dave and I backed against these doors and surveyed the scene before us. It was like the Colosseum in Rome and we even had the lions! As we secured our backs against these vast sheets of steel, we were both suddenly aware of the heavy ornamental door-knockers as they pressed into our spines. I made a mental note to beware of them should the crowd become too packed.

Possibly because of our slightly elevated position and also because of Dave's great height, we became a focal point for enquiries. The pavement is fairly wide at that location and slopes away appreciably towards the road. We had a fairly good view of the whole of that corner, and the multitude on the corner could also see us. The queues therefore formed. The most common request, approximately every fifty seconds or so, was, 'Where's the toilet?'

I do not know how the tradition of kissing policemen on New Year's Eve first arose but it is certainly a terrific idea. After dozens of passionate kisses, I received one from a frizzy-haired bespectacled young lady. I was astonished at her reaction. She stepped back and pronounced quite seriously, 'I do not approve of the police force. I think that they are fascists. However, you are all people, and I love people!' With that she again stepped forward and, throwing her arms around me, kissed me once more!

Nor was Dave without his difficulties. After three young nurses had finished with me, they moved on to him. Two of the three were no problem, but the third was an extremely small girl. With Dave being so tall and also standing a couple of steps high, she could not reach him. So her two compan- ions lifted her up for the statutory smacker. As they lowered her to the ground and went laughingly on their way, I noticed

Dave bend slowly forward. Within a few seconds, he was almost doubled.

'That must have been some kiss, Dave!' I commented enviously.

'Kiss nothing!' he panted, looking up at me with a pained expression. 'She's kneed me in the nuts!'

Ignoring his agony, I persisted with my own good fortune. 'I think I'm going to enjoy this evening, Dave, I must have been kissed forty times already.'

He showed by his reply how the knee to his groin had jaundiced his viewpoint. 'In a month's time you'll probably have galloping herpes!' That's a big problem with Dave – he becomes negative under stress.

At about half past ten, a beautiful Indian lady sidled seductively up to me. I sighed in anticipation. I had now become pleasantly accustomed to those perfumed and Bacardi-flavoured kisses. It had long ceased to occur to me that there could well be some other reason for an attractive lady to approach a mature policeman. I graciously offered my cheek.

'Do you mind if I stand with you? I have a bad leg,' was her crushing opening.

'Oh – er, yes, of course. Yes, please do,' I answered falteringly, making room for her on the steps with no small embarrassment.

She had, it transpired, recently undergone major surgery on her left leg. It was now encased in leg-irons.

'Why on earth did you come up here this evening?' I asked, once I had recovered from my original disappointment.

'I just had no idea that it would be so crowded.'

'But how are you going to get back home?'

'My friends are due to meet me here soon. I'll return with

196

them, providing that I can just cling on to you until they arrive?'

'Of course!' I agreed gallantly. As she clung intently on to my arm, I considered it more than a suitable substitute for a kiss.

The Indian lady's astonishment at the number of people in the square reflected itself in the attitude of countless others. Two smartly dressed Italian gentlemen asked me in faltering English, 'Why izza so many peoples'a here?'

'It's New Year's Eve,' I explained. 'Don't you have New Year's in Italy?'

'Wella course! But whazza gonna happen?'

'What's going to happen? Well, twelve o'clock'll strike and everyone'll go home. That's what's going to happen!' They looked at each other and shrugged as they fought their way back towards the Strand.

Threading his way towards us through the throng, I suddenly saw a huge man, equally the size of Dave. On his shoulders he carried a slumped figure. He grunted as he reached the steps and bent forward to jettison his load. The body rolled smoothly off his shoulders and down on to the base of the steps.

'Here y'are,' he panted.

'What's this?' I asked.

'Fainted. That's his girlfriend behind me. She'll tell you all you want to know.' I glanced quickly down at the still form. 'He's not fainted, he's drunk!'

'Well, he's nothing to do with me!' protested the carrier. 'I just helped his girlfriend out.'

'All right,' I sighed, 'but if he's not claimed within fourteen days then he's yours, okay?'

'If you can find me!' He laughed as he fought his way back into the crowd.

I turned my attention to the girlfriend. She was a pathetic wisp of a creature, with thin lips and a whining voice. She too had been drinking but she was at least coherent. It seemed that she had decided to stand by him because he was in possession of most of her money. 'Unless I can go through his pockets and take it back?' she suggested. I was very tempted to permit this but on reflection realized I would be the idiot of the night if she turned out to be his someone other than girlfriend.

'No, sorry, luv. But if you stay around until he comes to, I'll ask him for your money.'

Dave and I bent over him to make him as comfortable as we could, when yet another unconscious figure fell over us. This time it was a girl. Her boyfriend was in total panic. Off-duty nurses were everywhere in the square. When they were not kissing policemen, they attended to the sick, lame and drunk. Two now appeared out of nowhere. They gave Dave and I a big kiss each and attended to our latest casualty.

The panic-stricken boyfriend was rapidly becoming a pest. He kept trying to pull the girl to her feet. When that did not work, he tried to lie her down. We already had more than enough problems with our male drunk. He would occasionally roll away from our steps and into the crowd. Each time we had managed to retrieve him but it was becoming increasingly difficult. In addition to this, whenever I left the steps I had to ensure that my lovely Indian companion was firmly secured to the door-knockers. I now decided it was time to speak firmly to the young boyfriend.

'Look! Leave her alone! The nurses will soon get her moving, then you can take her home. So just be quiet and behave yourself.'

'She's had too much to drink, too much to drink,' he kept repeating. 'Her dad'll kill me.'

I thought that was beginning to sound like a pretty sensible idea. After five minutes or so, the nurses slowly pulled our young casualty to a standing position. She had made a very good recovery. Soon after that, we permitted the boyfriend to put his arms around her and edge their way along the pavement. Presumably to his premature death.

If the pavement had been crowded earlier it was now practically solid. The two-way flow of people had almost stopped and there was still nearly an hour to midnight. The sheer volume of the mass seemed intimidating. Periodically a storm-wave of humanity would throw those of us on the steps back against those unyielding steel doors. Each time our drunk rolled off the step, there was a grave risk that we would lose him permanently. 'We've got to do something about him!' grunted Dave determinedly, as he barged his way around the front of me and knelt over the prostrate form. We decided to wedge the drunk between the bottom of our legs, in order to hold him in position lengthwise along the middle step. The only problem with this was that his arms kept falling out under the massed feet. The most amazing aspect of the whole situation was that so far he appeared unmarked. Unquestionably God takes care of drunks. We knelt down and tried to fix his wandering arms inside the tops of his trousers. Suddenly there was a blow on the side of my head and a cool wind ran through my thinning hair. I knew instantly what that meant. My helmet had gone!

I fought my way to my feet and could just discern a slim figure squirming his way through the packed crowd in the direction of the Strand. That direction at least had the advantage of being slightly less congested. I then saw the figure push back his arm in the motion of throwing. I knew that if he threw the helmet for any distance I would never see it again. This for me would be very unfortunate. First, it was the only helmet I had. Secondly, I might well have to pay for it, and thirdly we had been expressly instructed to wear our chin-straps down, to prevent just this situation arising.

I practically dived over the shoulders of the people in front of me. Just as the arm came up to throw, I delivered a hefty wallop to the thrower's ribs. There was a loud grunt and the arm dropped. I pulled the lad roughly back by his anorak and he fell on to his buttocks between my feet. I snatched back the helmet and bent angrily over the now squatting figure. Through gritted teeth I began, 'Don't you ever − ' I stopped in astonishment. My slim young man was in fact a lovely fair-haired young girl. She tried to tell me, with a distinct American accent, that it was not her who took it. I was too ashamed even to pull her to her feet. I rammed the helmet back on to my head and turned guiltily away.

In view of how quickly I had accomplished the chase, I was quite surprised by how long it took me to return to the doorway. Those few yards made a tremendous difference to the density of the crowd. There is no doubt that if my helmet-snatcher had run off in the opposite direction, neither of us could have moved. Once more Dave and I straddled our slumbering drunk. The Indian lady gripped my arm even tighter and we backed further still on to the door. Still the kisses showered upon us. We became so blasé about them that when three young men decided to chat to us I felt compelled to move them on. 'Sorry, lads, I don't wish to appear unsociable but you're stopping us from being kissed. At my age I cannot afford to waste such opportunities!'

Eventually the New Year slipped in. It certainly was never proclaimed. The continual roar from the throng prevented any church clock, or even Big Ben, from being heard. The year in fact entered by courtesy of a number of unofficial announcements from assorted corners of the square. I

200

wondered what my Italians were making of it all! For a few minutes, no one appeared to want to move. They just wanted to drench themselves in the spirit of bonhomie — a spirit that would doubtless desert them just as soon as they awoke next morning.

The continual roar of the crowd had now given way to cheers and people began to sing 'Auld Lang Syne'. Although many could link arms, they were far too packed to pump them up and down. Kisses, embraces, the first line of songs, undying love and good fellowship were everywhere.

'Please, please help me!' sobbed the young American lady. 'I've had my handbag stolen!'

'Did you have much in it, luv?' I asked, anxiously. I could see in her eyes that she did.

Her lips trembled yet she held back the tears long enough to blurt out, 'Two hundred pounds, my travellers cheques, all of my credit cards, passport and marriage certificate, just about everything that I possess.' She closed her eyes, bit her lips and swayed. Her female companion hastily held her. I wanted to be sympathetic, yet my first instinct was to shake her and scream 'Why?' at her. 'Why did you take all of that property into a crowd? Why didn't you lock it in your hotel? Why do you carry so much around with you at this time of night?' Instead, I compromised, slowly shook my head and said uselessly patronizing words like, 'You are a silly girl, you know, you should have left it in your hotel.' I wanted to put my arms around her and tell her that everything would get better and that we would soon find all her property. I knew, of course, that we wouldn't. Her robber would be far away now, no doubt gloating over his haul. His delight at his success would not match one-hundredth part of her misery at her loss.

'I wasn't going to take it with me,' she sobbed, almost

apologetically. 'I really wasn't — but then I changed my mind.' With that, the dam finally broke and the tears cascaded down her face. It is on occasions such as this that I could happily kill bag-snatchers. I took a few particulars and then sent her to the mobile police office on the south side of the square. There was just an outside chance that she might regain her marriage certificate, though I doubted it.

It was now some minutes after midnight, yet the crowd had not noticeably thinned. A sudden burst of people exploded against us and my Indian friend turned her face into my shoulder and hid. This was easily the worst surge that we had experienced so far. I was aware of the iron door-knocker boring its way into my spine. I tried to move away from its bone-cracking pressure but my movement was completely restricted by the massed bodies around me. The crowd became even tighter and heavier as I arched my back to allow my shoulder blades to take the pressure off my breaking spine. The pain had reached an intolerable level when I heard myself yell. I pushed forward instinctively and pummelled the people immediately in front of me.

The tide suddenly eased back, almost as quickly as it had surged forward. I looked to my right at Dave and breathed a few great sighs of relief. He had obviously found himself in a similar position. The Indian lady was buried somewhere underneath my left arm-pit. Our drunk had slept on, safely anchored between our legs and totally unscathed.

'Can I have him back yet?' whined a slightly familiar voice. I looked to my left and saw the girlfriend of the sleeping inebriate. I had totally forgotten about her! 'Well yes, if you can wake him, be our guest,' I offered.

The three of us bent down once more over him. Yet again I anchored my Asian friend to the door-knocker. We shook him and slapped his face a little and slowly he woke.

'Get me a taxi!' he demanded.

'You won't be able to get a taxi for ages yet,' Dave told him.

'Then I'll go back to sleep till I can,' he announced. With that, he turned on his side and closed his eyes.

'What the hell are we going to do with him?' asked Dave.

'Well, the crowd does seem to be thinning just a little,' I observed. 'We'll prop him up and perhaps this young lady will keep an eye on him, will you?' I asked her.

'I've got to, haven't I? He's got my bleeding money!'

I rose to my feet and realized that the Indian lady was still clinging grimly to the door-knocker.

'I should think you can leave go now. The worst of the crush seems to be over.'

'Yes, thank you very much. I think that I can make my way back to my friends now. May I give you both a New Year kiss?'

'You didn't think that you were going to escape without doing so?' I countered.

'Well, in that case, I have no choice,' she smiled. Having dispatched a pair of warm kisses to a pair of warm coppers, she limped away into the rapidly thinning crowd.

'Well, I should think that's about it, Dave. We should be away nice and early tonight. About half an hour will see this lot finished. Hullo! What's he want?' My attention had been attracted to a grim-faced uniformed inspector, who was making his way straight towards us.

'Blimey, he doesn't look very happy,' exclaimed Dave. 'What've you done?'

'You men! Quickly, this way!' The inspector then turned back in the direction from which he had come and obviously expected us to follow him.

When we reached the centre of the road, we saw several

other policemen there. A chief inspector approached us. 'Okay, form a cordon across the road, no one is to pass through. I want that centre kept completely clear.'

'What's happened, sir?' I asked him.

'Two women were killed in the crush. They seemed to have fallen down and were trampled underfoot.'

'Where?' I exclaimed, incredulously.

'Just there.' He pointed to a spot in the roadway.

I looked up towards our vacated doorway. I found it unbelievable. It was not twenty-five yards away from where we were standing and we had been totally unaware of it.

There is a problem with forming a cordon in such circumstances. The public naturally wish to know what has happened. Yet there are many coppers who take an absolute delight in being secretive about something as open as two public deaths in a crowded square. By the same token, there are many members of the public who are a total pain in the neck. They will fight to have a closer look, revel in every last gory detail and even pick up some blood-stained ghoulish souvenir. Within a few minutes our cordon was practically shoulder to shoulder. Yet still we had difficulty preventing the occasional voyeur from struggling through our ranks.

Inside the cordon was the pathetic debris of a large crowd. Gloves, hats, scarves, crushed tins, sweet-wrappers, broken jewellery, broken glass and odd shoes. It was these individual shoes that somehow seemed the saddest items of all. One tearful sixteen-year-old girl asked me to retrieve her shoe from just inside the cordon. Her unshod stockinged foot was already bleeding, and damp from the moist night air. I could not see any great reason to deny her this. There was so much rubbish lying around within the cordon that I could not see one shoe making very much difference. I leaned forward to reach out and remove it.

'What are you doing?' called out an apparently senior-ranked, plain-clothes police officer.

'I'm getting her shoe. Her foot's bleeding and she has a long way to go home,' I explained.

'I can't help that! There have been two people killed here tonight. Put beside that, a shoe is very small beer indeed. Take her name and address and we'll forward it on to her.'

'I don't think that I want to do that, sir. Perhaps you'll do it instead.' To his credit, he did, and without another word to me. If it had been a murder scene I would, of course, have felt differently. But an accident in the middle of the road, with masses of items lying everywhere, did not constitute for me sufficient reason why a sixteen-year-old girl should need to traipse halfway across London in the early hours of the morning with just one shoe.

Soon heavy metal barriers were transferred from other parts of the square and took the place of the police cordon. Broad white lines of marking tape were then stretched across this area in both directions. This had the effect of zoning the whole area into one-yard squares. Half a dozen policemen then began the task of transferring the debris from each small square into a heavy plastic bag. One bag per square, with each bag numbered. My colleagues and I were now more or less redundant. Even ghouls find little reward in arguing with mute steel barriers. Soon the official police photographers arrived and we adjourned into small chattering groups.

Although it was now nearing three in the morning, there were still several hundred people around in the square. The females among them were still kissing policemen but the magic had long gone.

At three-thirty, most of the police had been sent into the Mall to await the arrival of their coaches. This hopefully would be the last lap of the night. Two of our young constables had now rejoined us from nearby Cannon Row Police Station. They had been engaged there for the last two hours with an arrest for assault. Arresting people on occasions such as this can cause severe muttering. Everyone on the coach wants to get away as quickly as possible. Therefore any copper who keeps them waiting while he is engaged with an arrest, particularly one that he could have avoided, is not popular. It was this attitude that set the scene for the last act of the night.

About six groups of police, some twenty coppers per group, were gathered along the north side of the Mall. In the road, a double-line of ambulances was still parked along the centre of that wide carriageway. A small generator pumped noisily away by the kerbside. This machinery had an extremely important function. It powered the police refreshment trailer. Our hot pies would have been sad indeed without it. Wandering along the pavement from the direction of Buckingham Palace, came a drunk. This man was, however, no ordinary drunk. Drunks I have seen. I know when they are drunk and when they are faking. This man was a class one, a never-to-be-beaten, all-time-winner of a drunk. The one thing that set him aside from the minions was his superb sense of balance: this man defied gravity! He was dressed in an enormous overcoat and a silly expression. He had an ability to swivel from eight different sockets, scattered throughout his body. He could have limbo-danced under buses.

He obviously considered that he had a great affinity with policemen, because on seeing us he smiled beautifully. His legs then swayed forty-five degrees to his right, while his torso, forty-five to his left. He spread his arms out wide and turned his palms towards us. For one awful moment I thought he was going to sing 'Sonny-Boy'. He then dropped his arms to his side and straightened his body up rapidly. This sudden movement caused a whiplash effect in his overcoat.

'H-l-o yell,' he said, or at least something like that.

Every group of coppers was simultaneously fired with the same idea – get rid of him! Our group, being the first in line, advised him to travel on to the second group, some twenty yards further along the pavement. 'They'll give you a drink there,' recommended some enterprising young soul. He leaned his body back and his head forward. He then took a sighting. He studied the group thoughtfully for a while and off he went – straight across the road. He threaded his way happily throughout both rows of ambulances, then came back where he began, with us!

'No,' we explained. 'Look, further down there. See them? They'll give you a drink.'

This time he swayed off in their direction, looking for all the world like a Bendy-toy. But his attention was drawn by the three-feet-high generator. This object absolutely stumped him. He had no idea at all what it could be. We believed he thought it was a telephone, because he crouched down alongside it and tilted his head to one side.

He then did a truly amazing physical feat. From a crouching position at the side of the generator, he sprung straight upright without a hint of a falter and pirouetted on one foot. The other foot he waved over the top of the generator and finally completed the full circuit solely on the ball of his left foot. He then collapsed himself down like a deck-chair, into his former crouching position. Storms of applause broke out from the assembled coppers. He then swayed in two complete circles, before taking a well-executed bow.

'Hey, I know who he is!' claimed one anonymous voice.

'He's an undercover agent from the Sweeney!' The voice then turned its attention to the performer. 'If you're a copper, show us your dildo!'

The drunk now smiled even wider and once again leapt up and pirouetted breathtakingly over the generator. I shook my head in wonder. This place is full of illiterates: the hamburger salesman thinks a parasite is an umbrella and the drunk can't tell the difference between a pirouette and a vibrator. Sooner or later, our new friend was bound to do something even sillier. A policeman would then have no choice but to nick him. The arrival of our coach came therefore not a moment too soon. We clambered aboard and left him once again answering the generator.

Our coach crawled slowly around Trafalgar Square. It was now four in the morning and there was still a traffic-jam. Before we finally left the square and headed back to Wharf Road, I took my last look out of the rear window. The drunk whom Dave and I had left on the steps of South Africa House was now cuddled up to his girlfriend and they were asleep like Babes in the Wood. The street-cleaners were sweeping around the last of the revellers. The centrepiece was, of course, the closed section of the road. Sad little plastic bags stood sentry-like in each of the taped squares. A few passers-by gazed aimlessly at them. It looked like a big Christmas box-game, where nobody knew the rules. Was it really only four hours since the Old Year had left us?